BALANCE SHEET BASICS

SKILLS FOR SUCCESS

RONALD C. SPURGA

BALANCE SHEET BASICS

FINANCIAL MANAGEMENT FOR NON-FINANCIAL MANAGERS

FRANKLIN WATTS

New York   London   Toronto   Sydney

Copyright © 1986 by Ronald C. Spurga
All rights reserved
Printed in the United States of America
6 5 4

Library of Congress Cataloging-in-Publication Data

Spurga, Ronald C.
  Balance sheet basics.

  Bibliography: p.
  Includes index.
  1. Financial statements.   2. Ratio analysis.
3. Business enterprises—Finance.   I. Title.
HF5681.B2S63335 1986   658.1′5   85-26424
ISBN 0-531-15500-5

For Marie,
Kathleen,
Danny,
and Allen

CONTENTS

EXHIBITS

PREFACE

Today's managers are being called upon to make more financial decisions than at any time in the past. Hardly a day goes by without managers being called upon to speed up receivable collections, shrink down inventory levels or arrange bank financing. Since most managers began their careers in non-financial areas, it is only natural that they find these new demands for financial decisions somewhat bewildering.

The purpose of this book is to provide the non-financial manager with a basic understanding of how financial information flows are assembled to determine the operating health of the business enterprise.

In *Balance Sheet Basics*, you will be able to develop your financial skills by:

- Learning the basic obligations of the financial manager.

- Discovering the techniques for analyzing financial statements.

- Interpreting the profit-and-loss statement.

- Measuring the firm's liquidity.

- Using business ratios to measure the economic health of the business enterprise.

Balance Sheet Basics avoids technical jargon and provides the diligent reader with a "user-friendly" financial manual.

For example, in Chapter 2, you will be shown how to develop the profit-and-loss statement of a small manufacturer. You will also learn how to value the raw materials, direct labor, and manufacturing overhead accounts in order to interpret a profit-and-loss statement. Then you will be given a ratio worksheet with which to compare the current situation in your firm against your competition.

Chapter 4 shows you how to take control in financial management. Success or failure relates to how financial management manages. Measure yourself against the characteristics of proven achievers.

Chapter 8 presents a case history of ratio analysis in action. Discover for yourself the famous "case method" of financial analysis used for a generation at the Harvard Business School. And the remaining chapters show you how and when to put the "case method" into practice to turn yourself into a financial professional.

BALANCE SHEET BASICS

WHAT IS
FINANCIAL MANAGEMENT?

It takes money to make money. This maxim is a simple way of saying that a business must have financial resources if it is to operate profitably. If you are in retailing or wholesaling, you must keep a stock of goods on hand to sell. You need to extend credit to customers. A bank balance must be maintained for expenses such as paying suppliers and meeting payrolls. Unless you rent your place of business, funds are necessary for investments in land and buildings. If you are a manufacturer, funds are also required for equipment and machinery, for raw materials and supplies, for stocks of goods in the process of manufacture, for finished goods ready for sale.

But having money does not guarantee making money— that is, making a profit. You not only have to have money; you have to use it well. That is why financial management is important.

Financial management includes the following functions:

• Seeing that the assets of the business are used in such a way as to bring the highest possible return on the money invested.

- Evaluating the need for new assets.

- Obtaining funds to finance asset additions.

- Managing both old and new assets so that each contributes its full share toward the profitable operation of the business.

- Repaying borrowed funds from profits those funds have generated.

GETTING THE FINANCIAL RESOURCES YOU NEED

Your most important task as financial manager is to find sources of funds to offset the company's uses of funds. When a need for funds arise:

- You can increase liabilities and/or equity to match the increases in assets.

- Or you can reduce the investment in some existing asset so as to hold down the total investment in assets.

Let's assume, for example, that your business, in order to keep or expand its sales volume, needs to extend more credit to customers for longer periods of time. In other words, the investment in receivables (an asset) must be increased. You may or may not be able to increase your borrowings. That will depend, perhaps, on whether you can convince your banker that the move is a wise one and that the company's financial position is strong enough to warrant a loan. And you may or may not be able to get more equity capital to finance the receivables increase. You might decide, therefore—or be forced—to squeeze down other assets, such as bank balances or inventories, to provide the needed funds. Your job as financial manager is to decide which of these sources can and—even more important in many instances—which one should be tapped for the financial resources you need.

MAKING A PROFIT— YOUR BASIC OBLIGATION

A primary reason for owning and operating your own business is to make the highest possible profit for yourself. You also have responsibilities to employees, to customers, to members of the community whose lives your company influences—and these responsibilities are important. But it is you who have taken the risk of contributing capital. Your basic goal is to take care of this capital and use it as profitably as possible.

It is important, therefore, for you to have at your command a useful measure of business performance that emphasizes financial returns. There are several methods of measuring profitability, but one in particular—"return on investment"—is especially useful.

MANAGING ASSETS

One of your most important duties as financial manager is to keep the assets of the business working hard and productively. It is easy for a small business to slip into the practice of having larger inventories, bank balances, and other investments than are really needed. "Bigger" is often equated with "better." The sales manager wants larger inventories, more lines of finished stocks, more liberal credit terms. These added investments will improve his or her sales efforts. The production manager wants newer and faster

machines and tools, larger stocks of raw materials and supplies. These investments enable him to cut costs and meet
delivery dates. The financial manager wants larger cash
balances to make his or her job easier. Office management
needs new equipment. Often it seems that the opportunities
to spend money are unlimited!

The aim of asset management is to make certain that
new or increased assets pay their way. The added profits
these new assets bring in should total more than the cost of
the resources involved. The return-on-investment measure
mentioned above can be used to show the expected effect
on profits of an investment you may be thinking about
making. Thus, it is a useful tool in judging and comparing
various investment opportunities.

Often, unfortunately, opportunities that promise satisfactory returns on investment must be put aside because of
lack of capital. This is especially true in small businesses,
where financing new investments can be a real problem.
When such a problem arises, good asset management may
come to the rescue in two ways. First, it may improve a
small company's chances of getting a loan by emphasizing
to the lender the financial competence and alertness of the
would-be borrower. Second, additional cash can sometimes
be raised by reducing unnecessary investments in existing
assets. That is, it may be possible to provide funds for one
area of the business by avoiding or reducing their use in
other areas.

THE TOOLS OF FINANCIAL MANAGEMENT

If your financial management is to be more than guesswork,
you must have tools to work with. At the least, you need

accurate, well-organized accounting records, regular financial reports, and some techniques for analyzing the reports. These tools will not give you ready-made answers to your financial problems, but they will help in shaping sound decisions based on facts and tested principles of business management.

Accounting Records

Good accounting records are the foundation on which sound financial management is based. The reports with which a financial manager works can be no more accurate nor complete than the records they summarize.

Accounting records may be simple or complex, depending on the size and nature of the business, but they should be well organized and consistent. The small business that does not have such an accounting system would be wise to have a public accountant set one up and explain its use to the person who will be responsible for maintaining it. Today several service firms have developed "time-shared," computer-assisted accounting systems which simplify and speed up the process of getting good financial data on a timely basis. Many small businesses find such systems to be both economic and valuable as a planning tool. Your commercial banks can put you in touch with reputable firms in your business area so that the advisability of computerized bookkeeping can be checked out. Both time and money will be saved in the long run if you have a system.

Financial Reports

There are a number of financial reports that can be helpful in financial management. The principal ones are the profit-and-loss statement and the balance sheet. These two financial statements are important to you for several reasons.

First they are the basis for financial analysis; and as such, they are used by bankers and investors in making loan and investment decisions. If you want to enlist the support of these members of the business community, you should be able to provide the statements and to explain or defend items that appear in them.

Second, state and federal laws pertaining to taxation and financing require reports that can be prepared only from financial statements.

Third, you should be able to read and interpret these statements as part of your management program. Only through careful financial analysis can you find and strengthen the weak spots in your financial policies and plan sound and vigorous programs for the future.

Techniques for Analyzing Financial Statements

Various percentages and other measures of comparison have been found useful in interpreting financial statements and highlighting relations between their items. These comparative measures give us the ability to answer questions such as these:

- Could the company pay its bills if business conditions tightened up temporarily?

- Is the money I have invested in the business bringing me as much profit as it could? If not, where are the problem areas?

- What percent profit could I promise an investor if he or she put some money into the business?

- Are my inventories working hard enough?

- Does the record show that the business is strong enough and stable enough to qualify for a long-term loan?

Such questions are of interest, not just to the business-people, but to their banker, their creditors, possible investors, and others.

FINANCIAL
STATEMENTS

The two most important financial statements are the balance sheet and the profit-and-loss statement. The difference between the two is sometimes explained by comparing the balance sheet to a "still picture" and the profit-and-loss statement to a "moving picture." The balance sheet presents a financial picture of the business—its assets, liabilities, and ownership—*on a given date*. It is usually prepared as of the close of the last day of a month and answers the question, "How did we stand financially at that time?" The profit-and-loss statement (also called the income statement) measures costs and expenses against sales revenues over a definite period of time, such as a month or a year, to show the net profit or loss of the business *for the entire period*. Notice that the balance sheets shown in this chapter (exhibits 1, 2, and 3) are dated simply "December 31, 19—," but the profit-and-loss statements (exhibits 4, 5, and 7) are dated "*For the Year Ended* December 31, 19—."

THE BALANCE SHEET

The balance sheet has two main sections. The first section (the left side if the two sections are shown side by side) shows the assets. The second (or right hand) section shows the liabilities (or debts) and the owner's equity, which together represent the claims against the assets. The total assets always equal the combined total of the liabilities and the owner's equity (or capital)—that is why this financial statement is called a balance sheet.

Assets

Anything the business owns that has money value is an asset. The assets of a small business commonly include cash, notes receivable, accounts receivable, inventories, land, buildings, machinery, equipment, and other investments. They are usually classified as (1) current assets, (2) fixed assets, (3) or other assets.

- *Current assets* are cash and assets that are expected to be converted into cash during the normal operating cycle of the business (generally, within a year). They include notes receivable, accounts receivable, marketable securities, and inventories, as well as cash. However, if inventories are not to be used up (that is, converted into accounts receivable or cash) within a year, they should be recorded as fixed assets. The same is true of notes receivable and accounts receivable that are not expected to be converted into cash within a year—they should be treated as fixed assets.

  The balance sheet of a small manufacturer typically shows three types of inventories. The *materials and supplies* inventory consists of materials to be used in production, together with supplies used in connection with the processing. *Work in process*, as the name implies, consists of goods in the process of manufacture but not yet completed. *Finished goods* are merchandise completed and ready for sale. Finished goods (or merchandise) and supplies are usually the only inventory items shown on the balance sheet by small retailers and wholesalers.

- *Fixed assets* are those acquired for long-term use in the business. They include land, buildings, plant, machinery, equipment, furniture, fixtures, and so on. These assets are typically not for resale, and they are recorded on the balance sheet at their cost to the business, less depreciation.

  A fixed asset is treated as a long-term cost, with the cost allocated as depreciation over the working life of the asset. Thus, the value of a fixed asset shown on the balance sheet is not necessarily the same as the resale value of the asset.

- *"Other assets"* include patents, trade investments, goodwill, and so on. (Goodwill is recorded on the balance sheet only to the extent that it has actually been purchased.)

  Assets are also sometimes classified as *tangible* or *intangible*. Literally, tangible means "able to be physically touched." Current and fixed assets are normally tangible; "other" assets, typically intangible.

Liabilities

Liabilities are the claims of creditors against the assets of the business—in other words, debts owned by the business. They do not include owners' claims. Among the more common liabilities are notes payable, accounts payable, accrued liabilities, and allowance for taxes.

Current liabilities are those due for payment within a year. *Long-term (or fixed) liabilities* are debts, or parts of debts, that are *not* due for payment within a year. The *allowance for future income taxes* represents the taxes that will have to be paid on the profits of the current year, but that are not due for payment until later. *Accrued liabilities* are similar to the allowance for future income taxes in that the expenses are charged against profits of the current year, although payment will not be made until later. The most common example is accrued wages, which must be accounted for whenever the last day of the accounting period does not coincide with the last day of a pay period.

Equity

The assets of a business minus its liabilities equal the equity. This equity is the investment of the owner or owners plus any profits that have been left to accumulate in the business (or minus any losses).

If the business is incorporated, its books will show a capital stock account. This account represents the paid-in value of the shares issued to the owners of the business. Undistributed profits are recorded in an earned-surplus account.

If the business is a proprietorship or a partnership, the capital accounts appear under the name or names of the owners. Increases in equity as a result of undistributed earnings are also recorded there, as are decreases in equity if the business shows a loss instead of a profit.

Valuation Accounts

Depreciation and other factors reduce the value of some assets. Because it is important to state balance-sheet values correctly, the balance sheet is usually set up in such a way as to show that provision has been made for such reductions in value. This is done by using depreciation, or valuation, accounts. Some of the more common of these accounts are the following:

- *Accounts receivable* are analyzed according to the length of time the money has been owed. An estimate is then made of what proportion of them will turn out to be uncollectable. This "allowance for bad debts" is usually computed for a given accounting period either as a percentage of the average balance of receivables or as a percentage of the net credit sales for the period. The balance sheet shows it as a deduction from the asset "accounts receivable."

- *Losses in the value of inventories* may occur as a result of price changes, style changes, physical deterioration, pilferage, and so on. If such losses are likely to occur, an estimate of possible shrinkage should be made. This estimate appears on the balance sheet as a deduction from the value of the inventory.

- *Fixed assets,* other than land, decline in value. This decline in value may be due to wear and tear, technical obsolescence, and other causes. A periodic charge for depreciation should be made and shown on the balance sheet as a deduction from the value of the asset.

SOME EXAMPLES

Exhibit 1 shows a simple balance sheet. It represents the financial position of the Monar Company.[1] a retail enterprise, on December 31, 19—. Total assets of $165,000 are offset by liabilities and equity totaling $165,000. The balance sheet balances. The assets are grouped as current assets and fixed assets (Monar has no "other assets"). Current liabilities are identified as such, although there are no long-term liabilities.

[1]Not a real company.

EXHIBIT 1

Balance Sheet of a Small Manufacturing Company

The MONAR Company
Balance Sheet
December 31, 19—

Assets

Current assets:

Cash..	$20,000
Accounts Receivable...............................	40,000
Inventories	45,000
Total current assets	**$105,000**

Fixed assets:

Machinery and equipment..........................	$20,000
Buildings...	28,000
Land..	12,000
Total fixed assets	**60,000**
Total assets......................................	**$165,000**

Liabilities and Equity

Current liabilities:

Accounts payable...................................	$20,000
Notes payable......................................	30,000
Accrued liabilities	6,000
Reserve for taxes...................................	4,000
Total current liabilities.............................	**$60,000**

Equity:

Capital stock... $50,000

Surplus $55,000

Total equity... 105,000

Total liabilities and equity......................... **$165,000**

When the valuation accounts are included in the balance sheet, the statement becomes more accurate and therefore more useful. Exhibit 2 shows how they affect the asset figures that appear in Exhibit 1. Note the following changes:

1. Accounts receivable have been reduced by $3,000 to an estimated $37,000, all collectable.

2. Inventory values have been reduced by $5,000 to $40,000.

3. Total current assets, therefore, show a reduction of $8,000 from 105,000 to $97,000.

4. Machinery is now valued at $16,000 or $4,000 less than the original $20,000.

5. The value of the buildings has been reduced by $6,000 to $22,000.

6. Total fixed assets have thus declined by $10,000.

7. Total assets have declined by $18,000.

8. Surplus is now $37,000 and total equity $87,000, each one $18,000 less than in Exhibit 1.

9. Total liabilities and equity now balance total assets at $147,000.

EXHIBIT 2

Expanded Balance Sheet of a Typical Manufacturing Company

The MONAR Company
Balance Sheet
December 31, 19—

Assets

Current assets:

Cash		$20,000
Accounts receivable	$40,000	
Less allowance for doubtful accounts.....	3,000	37,000
Inventories.................................	$45,000	
Less allowance for inventory loss.........	5,000	40,000
Total current assets........................		**$97,000**

Fixed assets:

Machinery	$20,000	
Less allowance for depreciation	4,000	$16,000
Buildings....................................	$28,000	
Less allowance for depreciation	6,000	22,000
Land		12,000
Total fixed assets...........................		**$50,000**
Total assets		**$147,000**

Liabilities and Equity

Current liabilities:

Accounts payable...........................		$20,000

Notes payable	30,000
Accrued liabilities.........................	6,000
Allowance for taxes	4,000
Total current liabilities	$60,000
Equity:	
Capital stock	$50,000
Surplus.....................................	37,000
Total equity	87,000
Total liabilities and equity	$147,000

The balance sheet shown in Exhibit 3 has been expanded still further to make it even more useful. This is the relatively detailed statement of a typical small manufacturer.

THE PROFIT-AND-LOSS STATEMENT—A RETAILER OR WHOLESALER

A profit-and-loss statement of the Monar Company, whose balance sheet appears in Exhibits 1 and 2 is shown in simplified form as Exhibit 4. A brief explanation of the items is given here:

Sales

The item "sales" includes all sales of merchandise or services. The sales figure shown in Exhibit 4 represents net

EXHIBIT 3

Balance Sheet of a Large Manufacturing Company

Monroe Manufacturing Company[1]
Balance Sheet
December 31, 19—

Assets

Current assets:

Cash		$40,000
Accounts receivable	$90,000	
Less allowance for doubtful accounts.....	10,000	80,000
Inventories:		
Finished product..........................	75,000	
Work in process...........................	75,000	
Raw materials	20,000	
Supplies	10,000	180,000
Prepaid expenses..........................		10,000
Total current assets......................		$310,000

Fixed assets:

Furniture and fixtures	$10,000	
Less allowance for depreciation	5,000	$5,000
Machinery and equipment	$30,000	
Less allowance for depreciation	16,000	14,000

[1]Not a real company.

Buildings.....................................	$45,000	
Less allowance for depreciation	9,000	36,000
Land		15,000
Total fixed assets.........................		**70,000**
Investments................................		20,000
Total assets		**$400,000**

Liabilities and Equity

Current liabilities:

Accounts payable..........................		$40,000
Notes payable		80,000
Accrued liabilities:		
Wages and salaries payable..............	$4,000	
Interest payable	1,000	5,000
Allowance for taxes:		
Income tax................................	$16,000	
State taxes................................	4,000	20,000
Total current liabilities		**$145,000**

Equity:

Capital stock		$200,000
Surplus....................................		55,000
Total equity		255,000
Total liabilities and equity		**$400,000**

EXHIBIT 4

Profit-and-Loss Statement of a Small Manufacturing Company

The MONAR Company
Profit-and-Loss Statement
For the Year Ended December 31, 19—

Sales	$120,000
Cost of goods sold	70,000
Gross margin	$50,000
Selling expenses:	
Salaries	$15,000
Commission	5,000
Advertising	5,000
Total selling expenses	**$25,000**
Selling margin	$25,000
Administrative expenses	10,000
Net profit	**$15,000**

sales. It is computed by subtracting sales discounts and sales returns and allowances from gross sales.

Cost of Goods Sold

The "cost of goods sold" is the total price paid for the products sold during the accounting period, plus in-transportation costs. Most small retail and wholesale businesses compute cost of goods sold by adding the value of the goods purchased during the accounting period to the beginning inventory, and then subtracting the value of the inventory on hand at the end of the accounting period.

Selling Expenses

These are expenses incurred directly or indirectly in making sales. They include salaries of the sale force, commissions, advertising expense, out-freight if goods are sold f.o.b. destination, and so on. Shares of rent, heat, light, power, supplies, and other expenses that contribute to the company's sales activities may also be charged to selling expense. In small businesses, however, such mixed expenses are usually charged to general expenses.

General and Administrative Expenses

General salaries and wages, supplies, and other operating costs necessary to the overall administration of the business are in this group of expenses.

Nonoperating Income

Some small businesses receive additional income from interest, dividends, miscellaneous sales, rents, royalties, gains on sale of capital assets, and so on. In such cases the "net profit" shown in Exhibit 4 is really a net operating profit. The non-operating income would be added to it and any interest paid subtracted. The result would then be the net profit before state and federal income taxes.

Exhibit 5 shows, in more detail than is given in Exhibit 4, a profit-and-loss statement for a small wholesale business. The retailer's statement of Exhibit 4 would appear much the same if shown in similar detail.

EXHIBIT 5

Profit-and-Loss Statement of a Large Wholesaling Company

**Wald Wholesale Company[1]
Profit-and-Loss Statement
For the Year Ended December 31, 19—**

Net sales......................		**$666,720**
Cost of goods sold:		
Beginning inventory, January 1, 19—..............		$184,350
Merchandise purchases	$454,920	
Freight and drayage...........	30,210	485,130
Cost of goods available for sale		$669,480
Less ending inventory, December 31, 19—...........		193,710
Cost of goods sold.............		475,770
Gross margin		$190,950
Selling, administrative, and general expenses:		
Salaries and wages		$88,170
Rent............................		24,390
Light, heat, and power		8,840
Other expenses................		21,300

[1]Not a real company.

State and local taxes and licenses......................	5,130	
Depreciation and amortization on leasehold improvements	4,140	
Repairs.........................	2,110	
Total selling, administrative, and general expenses.......	154,080	
Profit from operations	$36,870	
Other income	$7,550	
Other expense	1,740	5,810
Net profit before taxes.........	$42,680	
Provision for income tax.......	15,120	
Net profit after income tax	**$27,560**	

PROFIT-AND-LOSS STATEMENT OF A SMALL MANUFACTURER

Because the small manufacturer converts raw materials into finished goods, its method of accounting for cost of goods sold differs from the method for wholesalers and retailers. As in retailing and wholesaling, computing the cost of goods sold during the accounting period involves beginning and ending inventories, and purchases made during the accounting period. But in manufacturing it involves not only finished-goods inventories, but also raw-materials inventories, goods-in-process inventories, direct labor, and factory-overhead costs.

EXHIBIT 6

Statement of Cost of Goods Manufactured
by a Manufacturing Company

Hayes Manufacturing Company[1]
Statement of Cost of Goods Manufactured
For the Year Ended December 31, 19—

Work-in-process inventory, January 1, 19—		18,800
Raw materials:		
Inventory, January 1, 19—.................	$154,300	
Purchases..................................	263,520	
Freight In	9,400	
Cost of materials available for use	$427,220	
Less inventory, December 31, 19—........	163,120	
Cost of materials used	$264,100	
Direct labor	150,650	
Manufacturing overhead:		
Indirect labor	$23,750	
Factory heat, light, and power............	89,500	
Factory supplies used	22,100	
Insurance and taxes.......................	8,100	
Depreciation of plant and equipment.....	35,300	
Total manufacturing overhead	$178,750	
Total manufacturing costs.................		593,500
Total work in process during period		$612,300
Less work-in-process inventory, December 31, 19—.......................		42,600
Cost of goods manufactured		**$569,700**

[1]Not a real company.

EXHIBIT 7

Profit-and-Loss Statement of a Large Manufacturing Company

**Hayes Manufacturing Company
Profit-and-Loss Statement
For the Year Ended December 31, 19—**

Net sales		**$669,100**
Cost of goods sold:		
Finished goods inventory, January 1, 19—..........................		$69,200
Cost of goods manufactured (exhibit 6)...		569,700
Total cost of goods available for sale.....		$638,900
Less finished goods inventory, Dec. 31, 19—.............................		66,400
Cost of goods sold........................		572,500
Gross margin		$96,600
Selling and administrative expenses:		
Selling expenses:		
Sales salaries and commissions..........	$26,700	
Advertising expense......................	12,900	
Miscellaneous selling expense...........	2,100	
Total selling expenses.....................	**$41,700**	
Administrative expenses:		
Salaries....................................	$27,400	
Miscellaneous administrative expense ...	4,800	
Total administrative expenses	**32,200**	
Total selling and administrative expenses................................		**73,900**

Net operating profit.........................	$22,700
Other revenue	15,300
Net profit before taxes.....................	$38,000
Estimated income tax	12,640
Net profit after income tax	**$25,360**

To avoid a long and complicated profit-and-loss statement, the cost of goods manufactured is usually reported separately. Exhibits 6 and 7 show a statement of cost of goods manufactured and a profit-and-loss statement for a typical small manufacturing company. A few of the terms used are explained below:

- *Raw materials* are the materials that become a part of the finished product.

- *Direct labor* is labor applied directly to the actual process of converting raw materials into finished products.

- *Manufacturing overhead* includes depreciation, light, insurance, real estate taxes, the wages of supervisors and others who do not work directly on the product, and so on—in other words, all manufacturing costs except raw materials and direct labor.

INTERPRETING THE PROFIT-AND-LOSS STATEMENT

Notice, in the profit-and-loss statements shown in Exhibits 4, 5, and 7, that the *gross margin* (sometimes called gross profit) is computed first, and then the net profit. The gross margin equals sales less cost of sales. It does not take into account the overhead expenses (other than factory overhead) of being in business, the selling expenses, office expenses, and so on.

The Hayes Manufacturing Company (Exhibit 7) reports a gross margin of $96,000 on net sales of $669,100. The gross-margin percentage, then, is about 14 percent. This indicates that the goods sold cost the company about $86 per $100 of sales.

The net profit of the business is the final profit after all costs and expenses for the accounting period have been deducted. The Hayes Manufacturing Company made a net profit of $25,360, or about 4 percent on net sales.

USE WITH CAUTION!

The balance sheet tries to present a "true and fair picture" of the financial position of a business *at the close of* the accounting period. The profit-and-loss statement tries to present a "true and fair" picture of the results of operations *during* the accounting period. These reports, constructed according to accepted principles of accounting, are one of the small businessperson's most important tools.

But they are drawn up under conditions of uncertainty, and many of the transactions involved are necessarily incomplete at the end of the accounting period. Also, the balance sheets do not reflect resale or liquidating values; they reflect the cost, or cost less depreciation, of the assets held by the business as a going concern. The figures depend to some extent on the judgment of your accountant who has decided which accounting techniques are best suited to your business.

RATIO ANALYSIS
OF FINANCIAL STATEMENTS

The two types of financial statements, the balance sheet and the profit-and-loss statement, are necessary—and useful. But they are only a start toward understanding where you stand, where you're going, and how you're going to get there. If you are to get your money's worth out of them (they do take time to prepare), you should study various relations between some of the figures they present.

A number of indicators have been worked out for this purpose. In many ways, these indicators or comparative measures (usually expressed as ratios) are more useful for analyzing your business operations than the dollar amounts. They provide clues for spotting trends in the direction of better or poorer performance. They also make it possible for you to compare your company's performance with the average performance of similar businesses. Some important points must be kept in mind, however:

- *Businesses are not exactly comparable*. There are different ways of computing and recording some of the items on financial statements. As a result, the figures for your business may not correspond exactly to those for the businesses with which you want to compare it.

- *Ratios are computed for specific dates.* Unless the financial statements on which they are based are prepared often, seasonal characteristics of your business may be obscured.

- *Financial statements show what has happened in the past.* An important purpose in using ratios is to obtain clues to the future so that you can prepare for the problems and opportunities that lie ahead. Since the ratios are based on past performance, you must use them in the light of your best knowledge and judgment about the future.

- *The ratios are not ends in themselves,* but tools that can help answer some of your financial questions. They can do this only if you interpret them with care.

MEASURE OF LIQUIDITY

Liquidity may be thought of simply as ability to pay your bills. It is the first objective of financial management. Measures of liquidity are intended to help you answer questions such as this: "Do we have enough cash, plus assets that can be readily turned into cash, so that we are sure of being able to pay the debts that will fall due during this accounting period?"

The Current Ratio

The current ratio is one of the best known measures of financial strength. The main question it answers is this: "Does your business have enough current assets to meet its current debts—with a margin of safety for possible losses such as inventory shrinkage or uncollectable accounts?"

The current ratio is computed from the balance sheet

by dividing current assets by current liabilities. For the Ajax Manufacturing Company (Exhibit 8), it is computed as follows:

$$\frac{\text{Current Assets}}{\text{Current liabilities}} = \frac{\$140,000}{\$60,000} = 2.3 \text{ (or 2.3 to 1)}$$

Is this a good current ratio? Should the owner of the Ajax Manufacturing Company be reasonably well satisfied with his or her firm's performance on this point? These questions can't be answered with an unqualified yes or no. A generally popular rule of thumb for the current ratio is 2 to 1, but whether a specific ratio is satisfactory depends on the nature of the business and the characteristics of its current assets and liabilities.

If you decide that your current ratio is too low, you may be able to raise it by:

- Paying some debts.

- Increasing your current assets from loans or other borrowing with a maturity of *more than a year*.

- Converting noncurrent assets into current assets.

- Increasing your current assets from new equity contributions.

- Plowing back profits.

Let's take some examples. Assume that a small business has the current assets and current liabilities shown in column 1 of Exhibit 9. If this firm buys $15,000 worth of merchandise on account (column 2) inventory will be increased to $35,000 and total current assets to $65,000. At the same time, accounts payable will be increased to $35,000 and

EXHIBIT 8

Combined Balance Sheets of a Manufacturing Company

Ajax Manufacturing Company[1]
Combined Balance Sheets
January 1 and December 31, 19—

	December 31, 19—		January 1, 19—	
Assets				
Current assets:				
Cash		$30,000		$30,000
Accounts receivable	$42,000		$32,000	
Less allowance for bad debts	2,000	40,000	2,000	30,000
Merchandise inventory		60,000		50,000
Prepaid expenses		10,000		10,000
Total current assets		$140,000		$120,000
Fixed assets:				
Buildings and equipment	$120,000		$120,000	
Less accumulated depreciation	70,000	$50,000	60,000	$60,000
Land		30,000		30,000
Total fixed assets		80,000		90,000

Goodwill and patents		10,000	
Total assets		$230,000	$210,000
Liabilities			
Current liabilities:			
Account payable	$30,000		$25,000
Accrued wages and taxes	10,000		10,000
Estimated income taxes payable	20,000		15,000
Total current liabilities	$60,000		$50,000
Fixed liabilities:			
Mortgage bonds, 4 percent	40,000		40,000
Total liabilities	**$100,000**		**$90,000**
Equity			
Common stock (5,000 shares outstanding)	$60,000		$60,000
Retained earnings	70,000		60,000
Total owner equity	130,000		120,000
Total liabilities and equity	**$230,000**		**$210,000**

¹Not a real company.

EXHIBIT 9 Effect of Various Transactions on Current Ratio

	(1) Original current assets and current liabilities	(2) Merchandise bought on account ($15,000)	(3) Cash paid on accounts payable ($7,000)	(4) New capital invested ($10,000)
Current assets:				
Cash	$10,000	$10,000	$3,000	$20,000
Accounts receivable	20,000	20,000	20,000	20,000
Inventory	20,000	35,000	20,000	20,000
Total current assets	$50,000	$65,000	$43,000	$60,000
Current liabilities:				
Accounts payable	$20,000	$35,000	$13,000	$20,000
Other	5,000	5,000	5,000	5,000
Total current liabilities	$25,000	$40,000	$18,000	$25,000
Net working capital	$25,000	$25,000	$25,000	$35,000
Current ratio	2.0	1.6	2.4	2.4

total current liabilities to $40,000. The current ratio will drop from the present 2.0 to 1.6.

Now going back to the original figures, suppose that the company, instead of buying more merchandise on account, pays bills amounting to $7,000 with cash (column 3). Current assets will then be reduced to $43,000 and current liabilities to $18,000. The current ratio will be increased to 2.4.

Working Capital

In neither of the above two instances will there be any change in net working capital (the difference between current assets and current liabilities). But suppose the businessperson of Exhibit 9, instead of taking either of these steps, invests an additional $10,000 in the business (column 4). This time, current liabilities will not be affected; but current assets will be increased to $60,000, the current ratio will rise to 2.4, and net working capital will be increased from $25,000 to $35,000.

Bankers took a net working capital over periods of time to determine a company's liability to weather financial crises. Loans are often tied to minimum working-capital requirements.

The Acid-test Ratio

The ratio, sometimes called the "quick ratio," is one of the best measures of liquidity. It is computed as follows:

$$\frac{\text{cash} + \text{Government securities} + \text{receivables}}{\text{current liabilities}}$$

For the Ajax Manufacturing Company, which has no Government securities, this becomes $70,000 divided by

$60,000 (see Exhibit 8), giving Ajax an acid-test ratio of 1.2 (or 1.2 to 1).

The acid-test ratio is a much more exacting measure than the current ratio. By not including inventories, it concentrates on the really liquid assets, whose values are fairly certain. It helps to answer the question: "If all sales revenues should disappear, could my business meet its current obligations with the readily convertible, 'quick' funds on hand?"

An acid-test ratio of about 1 to 1 is considered satisfactory, subject to the following conditions:

- The pattern of accounts receivable collections should not lag much behind the schedule for paying current liabilities. In making this comparison, you should think in terms of paying creditors early enough to take advantage of discounts.

- There should not be much danger of anything happening to slow up the collection of accounts receivable.

Unless you feel comfortable about these two qualifications, you should keep your acid-test ratio somewhat higher than 1 to 1.

A general impression about the current and acid-test ratios is that the higher the ratios the better. This may be true from your creditor's point of view, because they stress prudence and safety. But it is in your interest as owner of the business to be strong and trim, rather than fat. Idle cash balances, and receivables and inventories out of proportion to your selling needs should be reduced. The key to successful financial management is to conserve the resources of your business and to *make these resources work hard for you*. Two measures that are helpful to remember in this connection are average collection period and inventory turnover.

EXHIBIT 10

Condensed Profit-and-Loss Statement
of a Manufacturing Company

Ajax Manufacturing Company
Condensed Profit-and-Loss Statement
For the Year Ended December 31, 19—

Gross sales..	$303,000
Less returns and allowances	3,000
Net sales	$300,000
Cost of goods sold	180,000
Gross margin...	$120,000
Operating expenses...................................	78,000
Operating profit......................................	$42,000
Interest expense......................................	2,000
Income before taxes..................................	$40,000
Estimated income tax.................................	20,000
Net profit	$20,000

Average Collection Period

The average collection period, or number of days' sales tied
up in accounts receivable, can be computed from the balance
sheet and the profit-and-loss statement as follows (the figures used are from Exhibits 8 and 10):

Step 1

$$\frac{\text{Net sales}}{\text{days in the accounting period}} = \frac{\$300,000}{365} = \$822, \text{ the average sales per day}$$

Step 2

$$\frac{\text{Receivables}}{\text{average sales per day}} = \frac{\$40,000}{\$822} = 49, \text{ the number of days sales tied up in receivables, or average collection period.}$$

Knowing the average collection period helps you answer this question: "How promptly are our accounts being collected, considering the credit terms we extend?" It both suggests the quality of your accounts and notes receivable and tells you how well your credit department is handling the job of collecting these accounts.

The Ajax Manufacturing Company's ratio shows 49 days of sales on the books. To put it another way, accounts are being collected, on the average, in 49 days. A rule of thumb is that the average collection period should not exceed 1½ times the credit terms. If Ajax offers 30 days to pay, therefore, its average collection period should be no more than 40 days. The management should look into the reasons for the slower 49-day period.

The following variations in computing the average collection period are sometimes used for greater accuracy:

- Substitute the total *credit sales* figure for the total sales figure.

- Use an *average receivables* figure. (Add receivables figures for the beginning and the end of the accounting period and divide the result by 2.)

- Compute the average collection period on a *monthly basis*. Trends toward slower collections and serious deviations from your normal collection pattern can then be spotted quickly and remedied. Also, the monthly computation keeps seasonal variations in sales and receivables from distorting the picture. For example, the average collection period of a typical retailer would be overstated if computed on the basis of its annual end-of-the-year balance sheet. At that time of year, its receivables balance is abnormally high because of sales around Christmas.

- In figuring the average sales per day, use the number of *business days* during the accounting period—say, 250 days for the year instead of 365.

Inventory Turnover

Inventory turnover shows how fast your merchandise is moving. It gives you an idea of how much capital was tied up in inventory to support the company's operations at the level of the period covered.

Inventory turnover is found by dividing cost of goods sold by average inventory. The Ajax Company, with an inventory of $50,000 at the beginning of the year and an ending inventory of $60,000 (Exhibit 8), computes its inventory turnover for the year as follows:

$$\text{Inventory turnover} = \frac{\text{Cost of goods sold}}{\text{average inventory}} = \frac{\$180,000}{\frac{1}{2}(60,000 + 50,000)} = 3.3$$

This means that Ajax "turned" its inventories 3.3 times during the year—that is, it used up, through operations, merchandise totaling 3.3 times its average inventory investment.

Usually, the higher the turnover, the better. A high turnover means that your company has been able to operate with a relatively small investment in inventory. It may also suggest that your inventories are current and salable; that, since they have not been on the shelves too long, they probably contain few unusable items. But almost anything can be overemphasized, and inventory turnover is no exception. Too much attention to high turnover can lead to inventory shortages and customer dissatisfaction.

What, then, should your inventory turnover be? The desirable rate depends on your line of business, level of business activity, and method of valuing inventories, as well as on various trends. A study of the turnover rates of businesses similar to yours will help you answer the question. Past experience will also serve as a guide.

Inventory turnover is a much better guide than the absolute size of the inventories. Size can be misleading. An increase in inventories, for instance, may represent the addition of stocks to support growing sales. But it also might mean that merchandise is accumulating because sales have slowed down. In the first case, the inventory turnover remains the same or even increases; in the second case, it declines. Thus, if inventories begin to grow proportionately faster than sales, a declining turnover rate will warn the alert small business owner-manager that trouble is brewing. If inventories are increasing for sound reasons, the turnover will remain the same or improve.

Like the average collection period, inventory turnover should be computed monthly in order to avoid distortions caused by seasonal fluctuations. Records should be cumulative and may take the form shown in Exhibit 11.

Inventory turnover records for individual items, groups of products, and product lines are also helpful, especially for retailers and wholesalers. They show which items are selling well and which are slow moving. Such turnovers

EXHIBIT 11

Inventory Turnover by Months

	Inventory on 1st of month (1)	Cost of goods sold (2)	Monthly turnover[1] (3)	Annual turnover[2] (4)
January				
February				
2 months' average.......				
March				
3 months' average.......				
November				
11 months' average.......				
December				
12 months' average.......				

[1]Column 2 divided by column 1.
[2]Column 3 times 12.

should be prepared monthly or, for products that are perishable or become obsolete quickly, on a perpetual or daily basis. This enables you to reorder fast-moving items in plenty of time and to prepare to dispose of slow-moving items before their value depreciates too far.

MEASURES OF PROFITABILITY

Is your business earning as much profit as it should, considering the amount of money invested in it? This is the second major objective (after liquidity) of financial management, and a number of ratios have been devised to help you measure your company's success in achieving it. A few of them are explained here.

Asset Earning Power

The ratio of operating profit (earnings before interest and taxes) to total assets is the best guide for appraising the over-all earning power of your company's assets. This ratio does not take into account what proportion of the assets represents creditors' equity and what proportion represents your own equity, nor of varying tax rates. For the Ajax Manufacturing Company, it is computed as follows:

$$\frac{\text{Operating profit}}{\text{total assets}} = \frac{\$42,000}{\$230,000} = .18, \text{ or } 18 \text{ percent}$$

Return on the Owner's Equity

This measure shows the return you received on your own investment in the business. In computing the ratio the average equity is customarily used—the average of the twelve individual months if it is available, or the average of the figures from the beginning and ending balance sheets. For the Ajax Company, the beginning and ending equity figures are $120,000 and $130,000, giving an average of $125,000. The return on the equity is then:

$$\frac{\text{Net profit}}{\text{equity}} = \frac{\$20,000}{\$125,000} = .16, \text{ or } 16 \text{ percent}$$

A similar ratio uses tangible net worth instead of equity. Tangible net worth is the equity less any intangible assets such as patents and goodwill. If there are no intangible assets, there will be no difference between the two values.

Net Profit on Sales

This ratio measures the difference between what your company takes in and what it spends in the process of doing business. The ratio depends mainly on two factors—operating costs and pricing policies.

If your net profit on sales goes down, for instance, it might be because you have lowered prices in the hope of increasing your total sales volume. Or it might be that your costs have been creeping up while prices remained the same.

Net profit on sales is computed as follows:

$$\frac{\text{Net profit}}{\text{Net sales}} = \frac{\$20,000}{\$300,000} = .067 \text{ or } 6.7 \text{ percent.}$$

This means that for every dollar of sales, the company has made a profit of 6.7 cents.

This ratio is most useful when you compare your figures with those of businesses comparable to yours, or when you study the trends in your own business through several accounting periods. Comparing the net profit on sales for individual products or product lines is also useful. Such analysis will help you decide which products or lines should be pushed.

Investment Turnover

Investment turnover is the ratio of annual net sales to total investment. It measures what volume of sales you are getting for each dollar invested in assets. The Ajax Company will compute its investment turnover as follows:

$$\frac{\text{Net sales}}{\text{Total assets}} = \frac{\$300,000}{\$230,000} = 1.3$$

Return on Investment (ROI)

The rate of return on investment (profit divided by investment) is probably the most useful measure of profitability for the small business owner. Usage varies as to what specific items from the financial statements are to be used for "profit" and "investment." For example, "profit" might be considered to mean net operating profit, net profit before taxes, or net profit after taxes. "Investment" could mean total assets employed or equity alone. It is important to decide which of these values you are going to use in computing return on investment and then to be consistent. In this discussion, *net profit after taxes* and *total assets* will be used. For the Ajax Company, then, the return on investment is computed as follows:

$$\frac{\text{Net profit}}{\text{Total assets}} = \frac{\$20,000}{\$230,000} = .087, \text{ or } 8.7 \text{ percent}$$

Here's an illustration of the use of the return-on-investment formula: Suppose a small businessperson has a total investment of $250,000 in a toy manufacturing venture and $100,000 in a hotel. He or she wants to compare the success of these unrelated businesses. The toy manufacturing venture yields annual net profits of $55,000 and the hotel earns $25,000. The return on the toy investment is 22 percent in contrast to 25 percent for the hotel. Other things being equal, the hotel operation is more successful than the toy factory in terms of the return on investment.

Assume, now, that the next year, the businessperson wants to increase the toy sales from $500,000 to $600,000 and expects the net income of the toy business to increase from $55,000 to $66,000 as a result. In order to do this, the executive will have to increase the total investment in the toy concern from $250,000 to $350,000.

The net profit on sales will remain the same—11 percent. The return on investment, however will drop from 22 percent to 18.8 percent. These changes are shown in the following summary of the toy manufacturing operations:

	Original	**Expanded**
Investment	$250,000	$350,000
Sales	$500,000	$600,000
Net profit..............................	$55,000	$66,000
Net profit on sales (percent)	11.0	11.0
Return on investment (percent).......	22.0	18.8
Investment turnover (times)...........	2.0	1.7

Why did the rate of return on investment drop from 22.0 to 18.8 percent, when the rate of return on sales remained at 11 percent? The answer is found in the investment turnover. A company's net profit on sales may be high; but if the sales volume is low *for the capital invested*, the rate of return on the investment may be low. While the toy manufacturer's profit on sales remained at 11 percent, its investment turnover was only 1.7 the second year compared to 2.0 for the first year. As a result, the return on investment dropped from 22.0 percent to 18.8 percent. On the other hand, the profit on sales can be low and still bring a high return on investment if it is coupled with a high investment turnover.

The toy manufacturing illustration shows why it is important to look at return on investment in addition to sales volume, profit on sales, and absolute profit figures. The investment required to produce the sales and profits are important. The entire triangle of factors—sales, profits, and investment—must be considered in financial management.

COMMON-SIZE FINANCIAL STATEMENTS

Sometimes all values on the financial statements are reduced to percentages. Balance-sheet items are usually expressed as percentages of the total assets figure; profit-and-loss statement items, as percentages of net sales. A statement in this form is often called a "common-size" balance sheet or profit-and-loss statement.

This type of analysis has little or no value, however, unless the percentages are compared with figures for other businesses in the same line of activity or with past records of your own company.

USING THE RATIOS

Ratios will not provide you with any automatic solutions to your financial problems. They are only tools—though important ones—for measuring the performance of your business. It is the use to which you put them that will determine their real value. Compare your ratios with the averages of businesses similar to yours. Also, compare your own ratios for several successive years, watching especially for any unfavorable trends that may be starting.

If warning signs appear, look for the causes and for possible remedies. Studying one ratio in relation to others may help here, but you will probably also need to look into the more detailed records of your business in the areas concerned.

CONTROL IN
BUSINESS
MANAGEMENT

What would you say was the most significant factor in the evolution of business management over the past twenty years? Would you vote for the computer? You'd have a strong point, for, twenty years ago, the computer was just coming out of its infancy.

Only a relative handful of those earliest computers were in use, and they were used mostly for statistical and mathematical computations. Today, of course, the computer plays a wide and universal role in business, not only in sorting and organizing data, but also in controlling production, making forecasts and diverse management reports, preparing payrolls, administering credit, and controlling inventory. In fact, the computer has applications for just about every aspect of business management.

Obviously, very few small businesses own or lease computers. Nonetheless, their electronic shadows fall on many small firms in the form of monthly reports from their banks, their accountants, or as computer-prepared payrolls or accounts receivable controls. But the computer is only a tool— the manager *controls*. And it is this control over the various aspects of business which has evolved most significantly in the past two decades.

This is not meant to discount the importance of sales and marketing administration. Nothing is more important than finding and serving a customer—as the saying goes, "Sales is the lifeblood of a business."

Sales techniques, however, haven't changed much in the last twenty years, whereas financial control methods have proliferated. Thus, from the late 1960s on, we have seen the emergence of a new executive position in top management of larger companies, the "financial vice-president." The position includes a variety of responsibilities, ranging from long-term planning and budgeting to overseeing expenditures, from supervising accounting programs and watching over profitability to making recommendations to management on all aspects of finance. In short—*controlling*.

And again, obviously, most small businesses can't afford to hire this kind of high-powered financial manager. The small business manager must wear many hats. As one such manager put it while attending a conference of small business owners:

> When I came here, my business lost the services of its Chief Executive, Sales Manager, Controller, Advertising Department, Personnel Director, Head Bookkeeper, and Janitor.

Small business owners have to be their own financial vice-presidents, too.

For large business or small, to be successful is, first, to be controlled. A business under proper control watches carefully every dollar that comes in and every dollar that goes out and understands how its capital is to be husbanded, safeguarded, dispersed, and how to keep a portion of its profits for expansion.

SUCCESS OR FAILURE
RELATES TO HOW
MANAGEMENT MANAGES

Why do tens of thousands of businesses disappear each year? Well, not only, of course, because of failure. Some owners simply decide to go into other lines of business. Others take on new associates and form new companies. Others lose interest or find they haven't got the dedication it takes.

On the other hand, an unfortunately large number are forced to close because their businesses are in the midst of bankruptcy, receivership, assignment, or reorganization under court supervision.

It's been said that more than nine out of ten business failures are caused by some weakness *in management*. This could be an overstatement. If a neighborhood grocer suddenly faces competition from a new supermarket opening across the street, or the largest factory in town closes its doors throwing many people out of work, or if fires, floods, or other acts of nature devastate an area, failure can easily follow. There can always be unpredictable circumstances that adversely affect the stability of a business.

However, in most instances, failures result from either the inability of the principals to manage their affairs or mistake in the way they handled their funds. In failure after failure, it's all too evident that the cause was ignorance, misjudgment, or other human error.

In 1975, for example, there were 11,432 businesses that went bankrupt or were otherwise insolvent. This was the largest total in eight years. These businesses owed more than $4 billion when they failed. This was by far the largest liability ever recorded for any one year—higher by 25 percent than the dollar liability figure for business failures in 1974.

By no means were these all small concerns. But, whether large or small, most of them failed because of inability to adapt to change or to *control* finances properly.

THOSE WHO SUCCEED

What about the other side of the coin? What about those who make good?

Let's emphasize one thing first: business success doesn't always depend on the amount of starting capital. One of the largest and most successful building material manufacturing firms in America was started just before the Great Depression by a motivated entrepreneur with just $500. This kind of success is still possible.

Yet, because of its capital position, it's common to think that small business is always at a disadvantage. The facts argue otherwise. Sure, large business has the advantage of strong capital reserves and specialized staffs for research and promotion—but small business has the compensating advantages of simplicity and flexibility. One recalls the remarks of the president of a small western New York steel mill:

> If we get a complaint, or a customer calls us about a problem, I am in the customer's office the next morning with my sales manager and maybe one of our technical men. By the time one of our larger competitors would have begun to study the problem or appointed a committee to look into it, we have already solved the problem or taken care of the complaint and maybe walked off with another order.

But to succeed a small business must be able to use its advantages. To exploit them, the owner-manager must be:

- Competent in production and marketing.

- Service minded.

- Motivated and hard working.

- Able to *control* financial affairs.

And so, here we are back at that word—CONTROL—the key to successful management.

Small business managers usually do have a good knowledge of how to get production and sales. Indeed, they could hardly have gone into business without such capability. But many owner-managers educated in the "school of hard knocks" need to build onto that training an understanding of the following fundamentals:

- Correct allocation of expense and overhead items.

- Sound credit policies and practices.

- Effective inventory control, both in relation to sales and to the operating capital in the business.

- Proper balance of assets, such as real estate, machinery, and equipment to capital.

- Intelligent management of both current and long term liabilities.

- Reasonable apportionment of earnings among competing demands, such as future growth and executive salaries.

To help the business owner are two fundamental control devices for guiding management: the balance sheet and the profit-and-loss (P & L or income) statement. Subsequent chapters will show how maximum use can be made of these devices through ratio analysis.

5

BUSINESS RATIOS
AND HOW THEY WORK

A balance sheet tells how a business stands at one given moment in the business year. A profit-and loss statement sums up the results of operations over a period of time.

In themselves, these two types of financial documents are a collection of mute figures. But when the assorted financial symbols are interpreted and evaluated, they begin to talk.

A single balance sheet is like the opening chapters of a book—it gives the initial setting. Thus, one balance sheet will show how the capital is distributed, how much is in the various accounts, and how much surplus of assets over liabilities exists. A lone profit-and-loss statement indicates the sales volume for a given period, the amount of costs incurred, and the amount earned after allowing for all costs.

When a series of balance sheets for regularly related intervals, such as fiscal or calendar year-ends, is arranged in vertical columns so that related items may be compared, the changes in these items begin to disclose trends. The comparative balance sheets are no longer snapshots, but become X-ray photos of the skeletal structure of all basic management actions and decisions.

Thus, decisions to increase basic inventories because of upward price changes may be revealed in larger quantities of merchandise on hand from one period to the next. If credits are relaxed and collections slow up when sales remain constant, there may be a successive increase in receivables. If expansion is undertaken, debts may run higher; and if losses are sustained, net worth declines.

Similarly, comparative profit-and-loss statements reveal significant changes in what took place. Were prices cut to meet competition? Then look for a lower gross profit—unless purchasing costs were reduced proportionately. Did sales go up? If so, what about expenses? Did they remain proportionate? Was more money spent on office help? Where did the money come from? How about fixed overhead? Was it controlled? It's only by comparing operating income and cost account items from one period to another that revealing answers are found.

STATEMENTS REVEAL IMPORTANT RELATIONSHIPS

In order to make comparisons meaningful, it's helpful to use relationships. If inventories are increased $50,000, for instance, the significance is difficult to evaluate unless the item is compared with sales and working capital. In other words, could the business really afford that much addition to stock? Did the merchandise turn over as fast as it did formerly? Or was the result an accumulation of unsalable goods? Thus, you need to relate asset and liability items to something else to make their significance easy to grasp.

Similarly, when you analzye costs in relation to sales, you can translate the cost figures into percentages of the sales. Then, by comparing the percentages from one period to another, you can see whether or not aggregate dollar totals of individual items meant progress or setbacks. Hence, profit-and-loss statements prepared by accountants show not only dollar totals, but usually also the percentages of sales represented by each item. Percentages, of course, are expressions of arithmetical proportions. And *Proportions are ratios*.

THREE KINDS OF RATIOS

Broadly speaking, there are three kinds of ratios. The first are balance sheet ratios which refer to relationships between various balance sheet items. The second are the operating ratios which show the relationships of expense items to net sales. The third group is made up of ratios which show the relationship between an item in the profit-and-loss statement and one on the balance sheet.

TEN KEY RATIOS

How many different ratios are significant? As might be expected, there's considerable difference of opinion on this question among experts. An early authority, Alexander Wall, while secretary and treasurer of Robert Morris Associates, listed 10 ratios in his book, *Basic Financial Statement Analysis*. Roy A. Foulke, another pioneer, concluded that there are 14 important ratios. On the other hand, a study by the American Society of Association Executives, made a number of years ago, found 34 separate types of financial ratios being compiled by 26 different trade associations.

That study suggested, however, that "It should be understood that the range of possible ratios is limited by the number and classification of accounts that are used in various types of business enterprises. Ratio study needs simplification. . . . Ratios may lose their significance and accuracy when they become excessively detailed. . . ."

Along this line, a primary objective in this booklet was to narrow down the field of ratios to a working minimum for small business use. Because of this, selection and rejection of material have been necessary. The following ratios, for instance, reflect chiefly balance sheet relationships. A few combine balance sheet and profit and loss items, while one, net profit on net sales, is based exclusively on data from the profit and loss statement. The procedures for preparing an all-balance-sheet study follow the same pattern as those outlined for combined balance-sheet and income-statement analyses.

Against this background, then, the following ten ratios are suggested as key ones for small business purposes:

1. Current assets to current liabilities.

2. Current liabilities to tangible net worth.

3. Net sales to tangible net worth.

4. Net sales to working capital.

5. Net profits to tangible net worth.

6. Average collection period of receivables.

7. Net sales to inventory.

8. Net fixed assets to tangible net worth.

9. Total debt to tangible net worth.

10. Net profit on net sales.

Brief definitions of these ratios appear below, followed by specific examples using data taken from the balance sheet and profit-and-loss statement. Explanation of the terms of the financial statements used in calculating the ratio is included in the discussion of each ratio.

1. Current Assets
to Current Liabilities

Widely known as the "current ratio," this is one test of solvency, measuring the liquid assets available to meet all debts falling due within a year's time.

$$\text{Example:} \quad \frac{\text{Current assets}}{\text{current liabilities}} = \frac{\$151,468}{\$\ 76,968} = 1.97 \text{ times}$$

Current assets are those normally expected to flow into cash in the course of a merchandising cycle. Ordinarily these include cash, notes and accounts receivable, and inventory, and at times, in addition, short-term and marketable securities listed on leading exchanges at current realizable values. While some concerns may consider current items such as cash-surrender value of life insurance as current, the tendency is to treat them as noncurrent.

Current liabilities are short-term obligations for the payment of cash due on demand or within a year. Such liabilities ordinarily include notes and accounts payable for merchandise, open loans payable, short-term bank loans, taxes, and accruals. Other short-term obligations, such as maturing equipment obligations and the like, also fall within the category of current liabilities.

Generally, it's considered advisable for a small business to maintain a current ratio of at least 2 to 1 or close to it for the sake of sound cash flow and healthy financial condition. This is not necessarily a must—particularly if a major part of the current assets are in cash and readily collectible receivables—otherwise, "2 for 1" or better is a pretty good idea.

2. Current Liabilities to Tangible Net Worth

Like the "current ratio," this is another means of evaluating financial condition by comparing what's owed to what's owned. If this ratio exceeds 80 percent, it's considered a danger sign.

Example: $\dfrac{\text{Current liabilities}}{\text{tangible net worth}} = \dfrac{\$\,76,968}{\$135,880} = 56.6 \text{ percent.}$

Tangible net worth is the worth of a business, minus any intangible items in the assets such as goodwill, trademarks, patents, copyrights, leaseholds, treasury stock, organization expenses, or underwriting discounts and expenses. In a corporation, the tangible net worth would consist of the sum of all outstanding capital stock—preferred and common—and surplus, minus intangibles. In a partnership or proprietorship, it could be made up of the capital account, or accounts, less the intangibles.

A word about "intangibles." In a going business, these items frequently have a great but undeterminable value. Until these intangibles are actually liquidated by sale, it is difficult for an analyst to evaluate what they might bring. In some cases, they have no commercial value except to those who hold them: for instance, an item of goodwill. To a profitable business up for sale, the goodwill conceivably could represent the potential earning power over a period of years, and actually bring more than the assets themselves. On the other hand, another business might find itself unable to realize anything at all on goodwill. Since the real value of intangible assets is frequently difficult to determine and evaluate, intangibles are customarily given little consideration in financial statement analysis.

3. Net Sales to Tangible Net Worth

Often called "turnover of tangible net worth," this ratio shows how actively invested capital is being put to work by indicating its turnover during a period. Both overwork and underwork of tangible net worth are considered unhealthy.

Example $\dfrac{\text{Net sales}}{\text{tangible net worth}} = \dfrac{\$759,016}{\$135,880} = 5.6 \text{ times.}$

There is no particular norm for this ratio. Each line of business tends to establish its own, according to studies made by Dun & Bradstreet, Robert Morris Associates, trade associations, and others.

4. Net Sales to Working Capital

Known, as well, as "turnover of working capital," this ratio also measures how actively the working cash in a business is being put to work in terms of sales. Working capital or cash is assets that can readily be converted into operating funds within a year. It does not include invested capital. A low ratio shows unprofitable use of working capital; a high one, vulnerability to creditors.

Example: $\dfrac{\text{Net sales}}{\text{working capital}} = \dfrac{\text{net sales}}{\text{current assets—current liabilities}}$

$$= \dfrac{\$759,016}{\$151,468\text{-}76,968} = 10.2 \text{ times}$$

EXHIBIT 12

Balance Sheet of a Small Business

ANY SMALL BUSINESS, INC.
Balance Sheet
December 31, 19—

Assets

Current Assets:

Cash on hand and in banks.....................		$ 17,280
Notes receivable	$19,280	
Less notes discounted	12,000	7,280
Accounts receivable....................	$87,780	
Less reserve for bad debts..........	7,500	80,280
Inventories.......................................		41,540
Prepayment of expenses		5,088
Total current assets		$151,468

Plant and equipment:

Land and building	$57,980	
Equipment, fixtures, and furniture ...	19,200	
Less allowances for depreciation ..	15,800	61,380

Intangibles:

Goodwill	2,000	
Patents	2,000	4,000
Total assets...		$216,848

Liabilities

Current liabilities:

Notes payable (bank)............................ $ 16,000

Accounts payable (trade)........................ 41,288

Taxes payable 14,400

Other payables 5,280

Total current liabilities...................... $ 76,968

Long-term debt... 0

Total liabilities.............................. $ 76,968

Capital

Capital stock $100,000

Surplus...................................... 39,880

Total equity or net worth..................... $139,880

Total liabilities and capital.................. $216,848

Source: Dun & Bradstreet, Robert Morris Associates, trade associations, and others.

Deduct the sum of the current liabilities from the total current assets to get working capital, the business assets which can readily be converted into operating funds. A business with $900,000 in cash, receivables, and inventories and no unpaid obligations would have $900,000 in working capital. A business with $900,000 in current assets and $300,000 in current liabilities would have $600,000 working capital. Obviously, however, items like receivables and inventories cannot usually be liquidated overnight. Hence, most businesses require a margin of current assets over and above current liabilities to provide for stock and work-in-process inventory, and also to carry ensuing receivables after the goods are sold until the receivables are collected.

The importance of maintaining an adequate amount of working capital in relation to the amount of annual sales being financed cannot be overemphasized. And it is this degree of adequacy which the ratio of net sales to working capital measures.

5. Net Profits to Tangible Net Worth

As the measure of return on investment, this is increasingly considered one of the best criteria of profitability, often the key measure of management efficiency. Profits "after taxes" are widely looked upon as the final source of payment on investment plus a source of funds available for future growth. If this "return on capital" is too low, the capital involved could be better used elsewhere.

$$\text{Example:} \quad \frac{\text{Net profits (after taxes)}}{\text{tangible net worth}} = \frac{\$ 23,768}{\$135,880} = 17.5 \text{ percent.}$$

This ratio relates profits actually earned in a given length of time to the average net worth during that time. Profit here means the revenue left over from sales income and allowing for payment of all costs. These include costs of goods sold, write-downs and chargeoffs, federal and other taxes accruing over the period covered, and whatever miscellaneous adjustments may be necessary to reduce assets to current, going values. The ratio is determined by dividing tangible net worth at a given period into net profits for a given period. The ratio is expressed as a percentage.

6. Average Collection Period of Receivables

This ratio, known also as the "collection period" ratio, shows how long the money in a business is tied up in credit sales. In comparing this figure with net maturity in selling terms, many consider a collection period excessive if it is more than 10 to 15 days longer than those stated in selling terms. To get the collection period figure, average daily credit sales, and divide into the sum of notes and accounts receivable.

Example: $\dfrac{\text{Net (credit sales for year)}}{365 \text{ days a year}} = \begin{array}{l}\text{daily (credit) sales}\\(\$2{,}079)\end{array}$

$\text{Average collection period} = \dfrac{\text{notes and accounts receivable}}{\text{daily (credit) sales}}$

$$= \dfrac{\$107{,}060}{\$ \ \ 2{,}079} = 51.5$$

This figure represents the number of days' sales tied up in trade accounts and notes receivable or the average collection received. The receivables discounted or assigned with recourse are included because they must be collected either directly by borrower, or by lender; if uncollected, they must be replaced by cash or substitute collateral. A pledge with recourse makes the borrower just as responsible for collection as though the receivables had not been assigned or discounted. Aside from this, the likely collectibility of all receivables must be analyzed, regardless of whether or not they are discounted. Hence all receivables should be included in determining the average collection period.

7. Net Sales to Inventory

Known also as a "stock-to-sales" ratio, this hypothetical "average" inventory turnover figure is valued for purposes of comparing one company's performance with another, or with the industry's.

$$\text{Example:}\quad \frac{\text{Net sales}}{\text{inventory}} = \frac{\$759,016}{\$\ 41,540} = 18.3\,\text{times.}$$

Manufacturer's inventory is the sum of finished merchandise on hand, raw material, and material in process. It does not include supplies unless they are for sale. For retailers and wholesalers, it is simply the stock of salable goods on hand. It is expected that inventory will be valued conservatively on the basis of standard accounting methods of valuation, such as its cost or its market value, whichever is the lower.

Divide the average inventory into the net sales over a given period. This shows the number of times the inventory turned over in the period selected. It is compiled purely and only for purposes of making comparisons in this ratio from one period to another, or for other comparative purposes. This ratio is not an indicator of physical turnover. The only accurate way to obtain a physical turnover figure is to count each type of item in stock and compare it with the actual physical sales of that particular item.

Some people compute turnover by dividing the average inventory value at cost into the cost of goods sold for a particular period. However, this method still gives only an average. A hardware store stocking some 10,000 items might divide its dollar inventory total into cost of goods sold and come up with a physical average; this however, would hardly define the actual turnover of each item from paints to electrical supplies.

8. Fixed Assets
to Tangible Net Worth

This ratio, which shows the relationship between investment in plant and equipment and the owner's capital, indicates how liquid net worth is. The higher this ratio, the less the owner's capital is available for use as working capital, to meet debts and payrolls, pay bills, or carry receivables.

$$\text{Example: } \frac{\text{Fixed assets}}{\text{tangible net worth}} = \frac{\$\ 61,380}{\$135,880} = 45.2 \text{ percent.}$$

Fixed assets means the sum of assets such as land, buildings, leasehold improvements, fixtures, furniture, machinery, tools, and equipment, less depreciation. The ratio is obtained by dividing the depreciated fixed assets by the tangible net worth.

Generally, it is inadvisable for a small business to have more than 75 percent of its tangible net worth represented by fixed assets.

9. Total Debt
to Tangible Net Worth

This ratio also measures "what's owed to what's owned." As this figure approaches 100, the creditors' interest in the business assets approaches the owner's.

$$\text{Example: } \frac{\text{Total debt}}{\text{tangible net worth}} = \frac{\text{current debt + fixed debt}}{\text{tangible net worth}}$$

$$= \frac{\$\ 76,968}{\$135,880} = 56.6 \text{ percent.}$$

Total debt is the sum of all obligations owed by the company such as accounts and notes payable, bonds outstanding, and mortgages payable. The ratio is obtained by dividing the total of these debts by tangible net worth.

In this case, since there is no long-term debt, the result is the same as the ratio of current liabilities to tangible net worth (item 2).

10. Net Profit on Net Sales

This ratio measures the rate of return on net sales. The resultant percentage indicates the number of cents of each sales dollar remaining, after considering all income statement items and excluding income taxes.

A slight variation of the above occurs when net operating profit is divided by net sales. This ratio reveals the profitableness of sales—i.e., the profitableness of the regular buying, manufacturing, and selling operations of a business.

To many, a high rate of return on net sales is necessary for successful operation. This view is not always sound. To evaluate properly the significance of the ratio, consideration should be given to such factors as:

(1) the value of sales, (2) the total capital employed, and (3) the turnover of inventories and receivables.

A low rate of return accompanied by rapid turnover and large sales volume, for example, may result in satisfactory earnings.

$$\text{Example:} \quad \frac{\text{Net profits}}{\text{net sales}} = \frac{\$\ 23,768}{\$759,016} = 3.1 \text{ percent.}$$

ANALYZING THE PROFIT-AND-LOSS (INCOME) STATEMENT

Based solely on data taken from the profit-and-loss (P & L) statement, operating ratios show the percentage relationships of each item to a common base of net sales. These percentages may be compared with those of previous periods to measure a firm's performance. They also may be compared to the typical percentages of businesses in similar trades or industries when they are available. Such comparisons will indicate the competitive strengths and weaknesses of a business.

The items included in profit and loss statements vary from business to business. For example, some businesses break down their sales expense to show the costs of salesmen's salaries and commissions, advertising, delivery costs, supplies, and so forth; some do not. In the following explanation of the P & L items, only major items are included.

The following explanations briefly discuss each term in the accompanying condensed profit-and-loss statement (see page 66):

Net Sales

This figure represents gross dollar sales minus merchandise returns and allowances. Some accountants also deduct cash discounts granted to customers on the theory that these are actually a reduction of the net selling price; others credit the discounts to "other" expense. "Trade" and "quantity" discounts are, of course, concessions off price, and should be deducted from the gross sales. In setting up the profit-and-loss statement in percentages, the net sales are shown as 100 percent.

EXHIBIT 13

Condensed Profit-and-Loss Statement of a Small Business

ANY SMALL BUSINESS, INC.
Condensed Profit-and-Loss Statement
For year ending December 31, 19—

Item	Amount	Percent
Gross Sales.....................	$773,888	
Less returns, allowances, and cash discounts	14,872	
Net sales	$759,016	100.00
Cost of goods sold	589,392	77.65
Gross profit on sales.....................	$169,624	22.35
Selling expenses	41,916	5.52
Administrative expenses	28,010	3.69
General expenses	50,030	6.59
Financial expenses............	5,248	0.69
Total expenses	125,204	16.49
Operating profit..........................	44,420	5.86
Extraordinary expenses...................	1,200	0.16
Net profit before taxes	$43,220	5.70
Federal, state, and local taxes	19,542	2.56
Net profit after taxes.....................	$23,678	3.14

Cost of Goods Sold

For retailers and wholesalers, this figure is the inventory at the beginning, plus purchases, plus "Freight in," and less inventory at the end of the period. "Freight out" is generally shown as delivery expense, either under separate or other sections of the statement.

For manufacturers, there are various additional items to be considered. They include supervision, power, supplies, the direct costs of manufacturing labor (including social security and unemployment taxes on factory employees), that portion of depreciation which enters into cost of production, and many others.

Gross Profit on Sales

This figure is obtained by deducting cost-of-goods sold from net sales.

Selling Expenses

These expenses include such items as salaries of salesmen and sales executives, wages of other sales employees, commissions, travel expense, entertainment expense, and advertising.

Operating Profit

This is the difference between the gross profit on sales and the sum of the selling expenses.

General and Administrative Expenses

These expenses include officers' salaries, office overhead, light, heat, communication, salaries of general office and clerical help, cost of legal and accounting services, "fringe" taxes payable on administrative personnel, sundry types of franchise and similar taxes, and other expenses.

Financial Expenses

This item would include interest, doubtful accounts, and discounts granted if not already deducted from sales.

Other Operating Expenses and Income

Here might be included various unusual expense items not elsewhere classified, such as moving expenses, against which might be credited income from investments and miscellaneous credits and debits.

Extraordinary Charges (if any)

Such expenses do not occur very often, but occasionally unusual costs such as losses on sale of unused fixtures and equipment do arise.

Net Profit Before Taxes

This figure is the profit after deducting the regular and extraordinary business charges mentioned above.

Taxes

This item includes the federal, state, and local taxes paid by the company out of its earnings.

Net Profit After Taxes

This figure is the final figure showing earnings available for distribution or retention.

Exhibit 13 illustrates how a condensed profit-and-loss statement would be expressed, first in terms of dollars, then in terms of percentages of net sales. (Not all of the above items are shown.)

6

STANDARD OR TYPICAL RATIOS

How much rent should I pay? How much am I entitled to charge against income for my salary? What should it cost me for making deliveries? What's the average cost of doing business in my line? How much should I pay my sales force?

Hardly academic questions. They are asked by business owners every day, as they talk among themselves, or as they discuss business problems with association executives, bankers, and credit people.

NEED FOR MEASUREMENTS

On occasion, financing problems arise which introduce further questions. One of the most common is this one: "How much should my business earn on invested capital?" Others are: "I want to buy some machinery. Can I swing the purchase on my present capital, or should I invest more money in the business?" "My competitor's business is for sale; if I buy it, will my operating capital be enough to finance both businesses?" "How fast should my inventory turn over?" "What size reserve should I carry for bad debts?"

The availability of information by which a small business owner may measure performance is important. Indeed, yardsticks in the form of typical or standard ratios for different lines of business have caused many small entrepreneurs to make worthwhile reappraisals of their business thinking.

Some time ago, for instance, a trade association representing part of the contracting business held a meeting to discuss problems in bid pricing. A problem in bidding was placed on the table. Participants were given a set of specifications and material prices on a mythical job. The problem was to figure the costs and bid on the job at a price which would return a reasonable margin of profit.

Bids ranged from 13 to 31 percent above material costs. Meanwhile, a trained cost accountant had already predetermined that the bid margin should be 26 percent. Discussing the wide variation in the results of this exercise, an officer of the association said:

> Our people just don't have an adequate understanding of their costs. They can figure the obvious items which they handle every day, but they don't allow enough for their fixed and indirect overhead costs, which aren't recognized fully until they come to check up at the end of the year. Frankly, our membership has too little understanding of all the factors that go into making up a price. As a result, very few of them are earning a fair return. But today's study of these factors in an actual case was an eye opener. . . .

At the other end of the scale, a rapidly growing number of business owners has come to look at ratios as management tools to pinpoint conditions in their businesses which need attention.

GROWTH OF STANDARD
RATIO STUDIES

Ratio analysis is not an entirely new development. As early as 1913, the Bureau of Business Research of Harvard University conducted a study of the expenses of shoe stores. Since then, many more studies have been done by various trade associations, government agencies, mercantile agencies, banks, research departments of industrial and accounting firms, and schools and universities.

Recognition of the importance of good operating ratios will do more than any other present influence to standardize procedures and, thereby, to improve management results.

SAMPLING THE FIELD

The first step taken by organizations in developing comparative operating ratios is to get detailed profit-and-loss statements from firms in the line of business under study. Naturally, not every concern will turn over its figures, others won't have sufficiently detailed records. And some won't have kept their records in a way that can be compared with those of most of the other concerns in the line.

Of course, if all the firms' figures were kept in the same way and all businesses in the line agreed to furnish them, there would be too much information to handle practically. To get, arrange, and interpret the results would take too much time and be too expensive.

Statisticians overcome this problem by "sampling"; that is, they get information from a random number of firms located over a wide area. The concerns chosen are picked because they are fairly typical of the line in general. Therefore, what's true of the sample can be relied on to be pretty much true of the line as a whole, although no single firm will exactly fit the "sample" firm picture that emerges.

Selecting the size of the sample and the make-up of the individual units of the sample are determined by the use of various mathematical formulas, all too involved to go into here. The important thing to remember is that, when it's done properly, sampling works and gives reliable results.

OBTAINING THE FIGURES

Once a method has been worked out for sampling the line, the next step is to select names of concerns in given random areas. These come from lists furnished by an association, from mailing lists, lists of customers, reference books, or whatever other sources are available.

The next step is to send out requests to them for detailed profit-and-loss statements as of a given date. Sometimes, the surveying organization will request that the figures be returned on its own specially prepared forms to insure uniformity and comparability.

ASSEMBLING THE RESULTS

As soon as the information begins to flow back to the statisticians, the job of assembling and compiling begins. There are several methods of doing this, all of which yield some kind of middle ground figures which try to reflect as nearly typical a result as possible. Once these middle ground figures have been determined, they are often arranged in summary reflecting in percentages the overall situation for the concerns covered. In other cases, figures may be reported in terms of dollar averages so as to show, for example, typical dollar sales.

Often, the figures are also regrouped in terms of size categories, such as stores with sales volume of $20,000 to $50,000, stores doing $50,000 to $100,000 annual volume, and so on. Or, the figures may be regrouped to show differences according to area, or city versus country, or credit versus cash sales.

Finally, the studies usually pinpoint relationships of certain key items, such as dollar amount of owner's salary, or salary per sales person, or sales per square foot, average stock turnover, and so forth.

One overall summary of a cost-of-doing-business study is shown in Exhibit 14.

OPERATING RATIOS VS. FINANCIAL RATIOS

The number of sources that compile comparative balance sheet ratios is relatively small, as compared with those which conduct studies of operating ratios. Much of the information which is available relative to comparative balance sheet ratios is on larger businesses.

Branches of the federal government, such as the Federal Trade Commission and the Securities and Exchange Commission, have compiled various balance-sheet ratios on large corporations, and similar studies have been made by a limited number of schools and universities. A few trade associations have supplemented their studies on operating ratios in their lines with ratios on selected balance-sheet items. Banks make private ratio studies based on their own files, and use the excellent studies prepared for them by Robert Morris Associates. The compiling of comparative financial

EXHIBIT 14

Summary of Operating Ratios of
350 High-Profit Hardware Stores

Summary of Operating Ratios
of 350 High-Profit Hardware Stores

	Percent of sales
Net Sales	100.00
Cost of goods sold	64.92
Margin	35.08

Expenses:

Payroll and other employee expenses	16.23
Occupancy expense	3.23
Office supplies and postage	.40
Advertising	1.49
Donations	.08
Telephone and telegraph	.24
Bad debts	.30
Delivery	.47
Insurance	.66
Taxes (other than real estate and payroll)	.46
Interest	.61
Depreciation (other than real estate)	.57
Supplies	.37
Legal and accounting expenses	.31

Dues and subscriptions...............	.08
Travel, buying, and entertainment ...	.19
Unclassified expenses	.64
Total operating expense	26.33
Net operating profit	8.75
Other income...	1.65
Net profit before income taxes.......................	10.40

Source: National Retail Hardware Association

statement ratios has also been done for many years by Dun & Bradstreet, Inc.

The primary use of financial ratios is to analyze the monetary condition of a business. They reflect its health.

Operating ratios also serve very useful purposes. One is to enable a manager to allocate, budget, and plan. Successful business management makes use of them to begin each year by designating the percentage of each sales dollar that will go to salaries, rent, travel, general administration, and so forth. With such management by forecast, a business owner can control progress and, if things go wrong, make immediate adjustments. It is a means of forcing profitability.

Secondly, by comparing percentage-to-sales ratios derived by administering costs within a business with those compiled from a cross section typical of the field, the owner-manager can get a good idea if his or her operating costs are imbalanced. Then action can be taken to eliminate the imbalances and improve profitability.

RATIO ANALYSIS IN ACTION:
A CASE HISTORY

Ratios have many uses. They are useful in analyzing collections, in checking inventory positions, in giving guidance as to condition of finances, in comparing expense items, and in pinpointing potential or actual disproportions as reflected by balance sheets and profit-and-loss statements. Later, in a following chapter, there will be discussion of some broad principles and applications of ratio analysis.

Sometimes, however, it is easier to develop an understanding of application of broad principles when they are highlighted by a concrete example. For this reason, the following case is included to show the manner in which the use of financial and operating ratios influenced an actual business in improving its earnings and finances.

A CASE HISTORY

Here is the story of the Middleville Lumber and Building Supply Company. Middleville is not the company's real name. Neither are the names of the towns, nor the names of the people. But the following account is accurate, if fictionalized.

As the scene opens, Dave Jenkins, the proprietor of Middleville Lumber and Building Supply Company, a local retail lumberyard, is in the outer office of the president of the local bank. He is waiting to discuss renewal of a matured bank loan. At least, that is his minimum objective. What Dave really wants is to obtain from the banker an *increase* in his line of credit. At the moment, Dave is attempting to marshal some telling arguments that would accomplish such a mission.

Dave had opened the yard about twenty years ago. He knew building materials. Margins had been good, and as fast as lumber came in it was shipped out. There had been little need to worry about competition. Meanwhile, the town had been growing—and as builders put up new houses and stores, Dave's firm had profited. Dave's net worth had grown from year to year.

But lately things had been getting tight. There had been strong competition. Builders were asking concessions, and the Middleville company was hungry for new accounts. While branching out into adjoining territories, Dave had been cutting prices. Year by year, he was increasing his sales, but lately was not making much of a profit.

The bank had been helpful. It discounted his trade notes receivable, at the same time opening up a modest line of unsecured credit on his own signature. Somehow, though, word was getting around that "Dave Jenkins wasn't always meeting his bills to suppliers on time." In some cases, overdue bills were resulting in rather pointed reminders from the creditors.

In preparation for his meeting with his banker, Dave had mailed his financial statement and profit-and-loss figures to the bank. These, he knew, would be posted and compared, after which he would be called in to discuss the figures and make new arrangements. He owed the bank $18,800 of which $14,000 was on open note, and was already due.

Dave had written down on a sheet of paper the details of his balance sheet and operating statements.

As Jenkins gave these figures one last going over, Roy Tompkins, the president of the bank, opened the door and called him in.

Tompkins's special interest was borderline accounts. Through a judicious loan policy and sound advice, he had aided a number of the local businessmen to stay on their feet. A file drawer in the corner of the office contained a group of folders, kept under lock and key, in which detailed records were kept.

The banker motioned to his visitor. "Come in, Dave; sit down." When Dave was seated, Tompkins opened his desk drawer and pulled out a group of sheets containing columns of figures posted in comparative form. The lumberman guessed that they were his.

"Glad you came in. I've been wanting to have a chat with you for quite a while. Dave, you're a good salesman, and you know lumber. How well do you know your own figures?"

"I don't know, Mr. Tompkins. Most of the time, I'm too busy in the yard to go into the ledgers. I leave most of the details to my bookkeeper."

The banker waited and then went on. "Let me ask you another question, Dave. Why do you insist on doing business for nothing?" Dave was startled, and he began to flush. He had been expecting to be taken to task for the overdue note, and had thought himself reasonably well fortified with reasons. But the conversation was now taking a turn for which he was unprepared.

"I'm *not* working for nothing," Dave countered. "These last two years have been tough. I've been building up busi-

EXHIBIT 15

Balance Sheet of a Lumber Wholesaler

Middleville Lumber and Building Supply Company
December 31, 19—
BALANCE SHEET

Cash.................	$ 1,896	Notes payable, bank	$ 14,000
Notes receivable.....	4,876	Notes receivable,	
Accounts receivable	97,456	discounted	4,842
Inventory............	156,822	Accounts payable....	152,240
		Accruals.............	5,440
Total current assets.........	$261,050	Total current liabilities......	$176,522
Land and buildings..	46,258	Mortgage............	10,000
Equipment and fixtures........	11,458	Total liabilities ..	$186,522
Prepaid expenses....	1,278	Net worth............	133,522
Total assets......	$320,044	Total liabilities and net worth	$320,044

INCOME STATEMENT

	Dollars	Percent
Net sales	$727,116	100.0
Cost of goods sold..........................	582,420	80.1
Gross Profit on sales	$144,696	19.9
Expenses:		
Drawings...................... $14,544		2.0
Wages......................... 74,166		10.2
Delivery expense 10,099		1.4

Bad debts allowance..........	4,373	0.6
Communications..............	2,181	0.3
Depreciation allowance	4,382	0.6
Insurance	6,543	0.9
Taxes	10,907	1.5
Advertising....................	2,180	0.3
Interest.......................	4,000	0.6
Other charges	8,358	1.1
Total expenses	141,733	19.5
Net profit	$ 2,963	0.4
Other income	2,179	0.3
Total net income	$ 5,142	0.7

ness—you know that. Look at my history. I'm worth more than..."

"Wait a minute Dave. I know what you're going to say. But just look at your figures. Last year, you netted a little over $5,000. The year before, it was $4,500 and that was before taxes. You could have done better working for someone else. You made virtually nothing on invested capital."

"But how much *should* I have made?" Dave asked.

"You know, Dave, the amount of profit a concern 'should earn' on its capital is something of an academic question. Some say that the ratio of net profits after taxes to tangible net worth should be at least 15 percent. Some large businesses in your line expect a 21-to-23 percent return.

"I look at it this way: If you'd gone to work for someone

else, and invested in high grade bonds, you could have safely earned around 8 percent in dividends. That's—let's see, $10,400—more than twice your earnings before taxes.

"Anyway, let's be practical. Your net profit on net sales this year was less than 1 percent. Your state association of lumber and building material dealers reports that its studies indicate an average return for its members of close to 4½ percent on sales.

"Maybe, Dave, you've got all the capital you're going to need," said the banker, as he spread out the Middleville company's figures over his desk. "You know, Dave, I'm convinced you have been violating three commandments of financial management."

"Now, wait a moment, Mr. Tompkins!" Dave countered. "You know as well as I do, I'll never borrow a dime I can't pay back, or buy a two-by-four I won't pay for. I'm solvent. Look at my figures. I've got assets to pay."

As Jenkins broke off, the banker picked up the figures and continued, "Don't get upset, Dave. I know you're honest, and I know your intentions. If we weren't sure about that, I wouldn't be talking to you. I'm thinking of something else. The three commandments I mentioned are: Don't overbuy, don't overtrade, don't overexpand. Now don't you agree you've done all three?"

Dave hedged. "Well—what makes you think so?"

"Look here." The banker and the lumberman drew up their chairs. "Let's start with your balance sheet. You show current assets of $261,000 and current debts of $176,000. Your current ratio is 1.48 to 1. That's dangerously close, according to your association. The average lumberyard should show—at a minimum—a ratio of 3 to 1. Other studies I've seen indicate a prevailing median current ratio of 3.4 to 1. So you look low on current ratio."

"Now take your working capital—current assets less current debts. In your case, it's about $84,000. That's the money you would have left over, if you were to suddenly pay off all debts by liquidating current assets. It's the protective cushion you need to have in carrying your receivables and inventory. Last year, your ratio of net sales to working capital was about nine times. Experience suggests to me that four times would have been about right. Take your turnover of tangible net worth; by that I mean the ratio of your $133,000 in tangible net worth to $727,000 in net sales. It was nearly five and one-half times for the year. My observation is that it should have been a little more than two and one-half times. I'm basing that comment on some 'standard' ratios I obtained for the comparison. That's why I say I think you've been overtrading."

"What does all this standard-ratio stuff mean?" Dave interjected.

"It's simple enough if you figure it out in logical order, Dave. Overtrading with finances is something like speeding in a car. At 30 miles an hour, a blowout is an inconvenience—but at 80 miles an hour?" Tompkins paused to let the point sink in.

"Look Dave—what if one of your big customers goes sour and you have to write some big receivables off as bad debts? What if prices take a quick tumble and your inventory declines in value? What if building should suddenly come to a halt in this area because of a strike? How about your own health—what if you were to be sick? Suppose creditors demand their money?"

"Suppose..." and the banker smiled, "Suppose, Dave, we called your loan."

Dave glanced up quickly. "Okay, Mr. Tompkins, I see the point. How about the loan?"

"Let's think some things through first, Dave. We'll get to the loan—and we don't want to see you forced out of business. But let's understand this: a soundly operated business has the strength to sustain blowouts. Yours hasn't."

"Now let's examine this balance sheet again. Obviously, you need more cash. You have $1,900 in your balance right now. Your operating expenses last year were $142,000. That figures out to about $12,000 a month. You have less than enough cash to meet a week's overhead. I'm inclined to feel that a firm should have enough cash to meet two weeks' overhead, as a minimum, and would really be better off to have enough cash to carry it for a month.

"Next think about your receivables. Your daily sales are about $2,000 on the average. Divide that into $102,000 in notes and accounts receivables on the balance sheet, and you have an average collection period of over 50 days. Not so bad. That compares favorably with a 51-day median shown for other lumberyards by typical ratio studies. At least, you're not in the banking business with your customers.

"Well, that brings us to inventory. Your company shows a relationship for net sales to inventory of—let's see, divide $727,000 in sales by $157,000 in inventory—yes, that's right—4.6 times a year. How about that inventory, Dave? Any deadwood in there?" The bank president chuckled.

"Well, it's like this," Dave came back a little aggressively. "I took my inventory low. I wouldn't sell it outright for $28,000 more than what I valued it at. Why I've got $20,000 worth of roofers alone that are up 20 percent since I bought them. Of course, it'll take me several months to move that much, but they'll go for a good profit."

"I'm sure they will, and when they do you'll be looking for more bargains. Tell me, Dave, are you in business to make a profit as a merchandiser or as a speculator on price fluctuations? What will happen if you guess wrong?" Then rather emphatically, "You *will* guess wrong someday, you know!"

"But Mr. Tompkins," remarked Dave rather plaintively, "does a guy have to shut his eyes to a good buy?"

"No; not if he can afford it. You can't. You need that $20,000 right now to pay bills with, not to mention our note. My checkings show that you're past due with your note payment. Those roofers aren't arguing for you with your creditors. Let's face it, Dave. You are a perpetual overbuyer."

Rather vehemently, Dave protested. "But business is a gamble!"

"So's driving an automobile, Dave; if you were taking a trip to California, you'd want to make sure your car was in good shape. You wouldn't just load up on gas and oil. You'd have a mechanic go over your car carefully—checking brakes, tires, engine, electrical system, windshield wipers, and so on. You'd watch out for overloading, too, because you know that excessive strain might cause a breakdown.

"Right now you're driving your business under an overload of items that strain your financial resources. Your current liabilities comprise 132 percent of your tangible net worth whereas a 30- to 35-percent ratio is all that most companies like yours are willing to carry. And 44 percent of tangible net worth is in fixed assets.

"That tells a story, too. I know the purchase of your yard property two years ago was tempting, even though we advised against it. Sure you cut your occupancy costs, but think of what you lost in discounts you couldn't take. Suppose you had invested just a fraction of that money in a lift truck. You'd have come out ahead on expense and have saved yourself some irritation and worry in the meantime."

"Gosh, Mr. Tompkins," Dave mused, "this begins to look as though I don't belong in business. Is that what you want to tell me?"

"Not at all, Dave," the banker replied, "What I've been doing is spotlighting a few disturbing facts to help clarify your thinking. You've been trying to take a quick and easy path around some roadblocks. In the process, you got lost.

"It isn't your balance sheet or your income statement that got you into trouble. Your statements are merely end products of some questionable management methods. The key to your problem, and to a possible solution, lies in your methods of merchandising. Your profit-and-loss statement makes that fairly clear.

"Let's start by making some comparisons. In this file, I have some data about businesses similar to yours to whom we have made loans. I have averaged some of them to find out what the bank thinks you should be doing.

"Take, for example, your expenses. Item by item they compare favorably with the averages in this file. Overall, your total expenses appear to be low—around 20 percent. On that basis, your net profit should be more than the average 13.5 percent shown in my file instead of 0.4 percent. Where's the difference? On the surface, it looks like your cost-of-sales is too high."

"You're absolutely right, Mr. Tompkins," said Dave. "Main thing, I guess, is the difference in profit margin. How do those businesses in your file get the prices?"

The banker gave Dave a keen glance. "Doing much business with Bromway Builders over in Elmville?"

"Sure," Dave came back, "thousands of dollars a month."

"New account, isn't it? I hear they're pretty sharp buyers."

"Yeah, they're rough," Dave admitted somewhat hesitantly. "But they're big-volume buyers."

"How much business do you do with builders and industrials, and how much with homeowners?" asked Tompkins.

"We don't bother much with that little stuff. It's a nuisance to cut and deliver a dozen pieces of two-by-four, six pieces of wallboard, and a pound of nails. We deal mostly in quantity, with contractors and industrial accounts."

There was no immediate reaction from the banker. Then he said, "They tell me you take business as much as twenty-five miles out of town. That would build up delivery costs, wouldn't it?"

Dave nodded.

"I also hear that you're a bear on service, that you'll deliver a half-load to anyone at a moment's notice. I've seen your yardmen working overtime getting out deliveries. Sure, service keeps customers happy and brings in new ones. But there have to be offsetting compensations. Your trouble, as I see it, Dave, is price.

"They tell me you'd rather miss a meal than lose a sale. Some people say you sold a carload of dimension lumber to Bromway just last week for $10 a thousand above cost. That's a pretty small markup on such an item. Frankly, your competitors have been a little gleeful about it."

"But," Dave interposed, "isn't turnover an objective? Everybody is trying for volume nowadays. What about this business of 'Profits in pennies, volume in millions'?"

"It's a nice slogan, in its place," said the banker. "Many grocers can work on small margins, and their net comes out at pennies per dollar. But they move their goods daily and weekly. They aren't so likely to take inventory losses. They sell for cash, mostly. They don't have to invest very much capital in equipment. Their volume is steady. But when a company has to stock large inventories in advance of a season, has to carry receivables and so on, capital turnover can't help but slow down."

"Costs-of-doing-business seek their level in every line. They put a logical limit on how low you can price. Sure, if new methods of selling and moving goods come along— like self-service—then the reduction in overhead can be passed on to the customer. But if you sell a carload of dimension stock at 10 percent above cost, somewhere along the line a carload of other goods has to be marked up proportionately to offset your overhead loss. Either that, or you go broke."

Anxiously, Dave asked, "All right, what do you think I should do; give up?"

"No. That's the furthest thought from my mind. I don't think it's a question of quitting. You're too honest, likable, and hard-working. You know lumber and building supplies.

"Actually, what you and I have been doing is diagnosing some symptoms of sickness. Perhaps some kind of operation is in order. I've got a few suggestions that I believe will cure this patient—if you care to listen."

Dave's reply was quick, and relieved. "Sure, sure—I'll listen. What do you think we ought to do?"

The banker continued thoughtfully. "Thinking over your situation carefully last week, I came to the conclusion that only part, but an important part, of your troubles is financial. Let's tackle them first. You can use $40,000 more cash, right?"

"Right!"

"Very well," said the banker. "The immediate problem is the loan. I can't risk depositors' money by granting you a larger loan. But I think we can do some refunding. Your yard property appears to have appreciated in value enough so that we can consolidate the present mortgage and increase it $25,000. That will refund your $14,000 note and leave $11,000 cash. It means $25,000 in working capital. Now let's look elsewhere.

"Suppose you were to cut back some of that inventory—say $40,000. Could you manage without causing sales to decline as a result? If you could, it would bring you to an inventory turnover rate of about seven times. You already have some appreciation on that $20,000 lot of roofers."

This time Dave was slow to answer. As a merchant, he enjoyed being well stocked. He had been through some trying years when merchandise was better to have than money. A well-stocked yard gave him a comfortable feeling. But there *were* those bills.

Reluctantly, he came to a decision. "Yes, I guess we could."

"Well, let's leave that one for a minute," continued the banker. "I have one more operation to propose. I want you to give up that unprofitable Bromway account. It's my belief he's headed for trouble; he's working too close. And I believe one or two others on your books have got to start paying you a better price. It's a cinch they'd have to if they did business elsewhere. If they're worth keeping, they'll go along. In other words, I would like to see you slice $50,000 worth of unprofitable sales volume off your books. It seems like a sacrifice, I'm sure, but no operation is entirely painless."

That was a shocker. Jenkins had worked hard to acquire these accounts, even though the concessions forced on him had been painful.

Tompkins continued, "It means less capital turnover, but at no loss in profit. Also it means buying several thousand dollars less each month. So you might say that, in a sense, it supplies that much additional capital. Furthermore, it means carrying fewer receivables. Taken together, these items begin to get us closer to our objective."

Dave brightened a little. The picture was beginning to look more attractive. Living with a daily burden of debt had been no fun.

"Now," said the banker, "let's look at some profit prospects. It looks as if this do-it-yourself market is here to stay. It's small, package stuff, but it can be profitable. All over the country, lumberyards have shifted their operations to take advantage of consumer business. They have put in paint and hardware, renting power tools, and so on.

"Over in Elmville, Chuck Stebbins is grossing 30 percent on that type of business. He offsets delivery costs by adding service charges. His power-tool-rental income paid for his outlay the first year. That's not so small, you know. Families are outgrowing new homes as fast as they move in; it means new rooms to build, improvements to make— rumpus-rooms in basements, bedrooms in attics. A good many of these projects qualify for home improvement loans. The bank will take off your hands all that kind of paper you can get.

"This generation of homeowners is a new breed. More leisure hours are resulting in time spent building garages, patios, and repairs. When these people buy, they want two things: service and quality. They'll spend money to get them. If you look at the facts carefully, you'll spend money to get them. Actually, 65 percent of the lumber and building supply businesses now consider themselves full-service dealers. If you look at the facts carefully, you'll see that there's money to be made in the consumer business."

As Tompkins spoke, Dave was already beginning to make calculations.

The banker continued. "This whole proposition must raise a lot of questions in your mind. Don't try to settle it overnight. Why don't you go back to your office and do some figuring. Draw up a budget and work up a few plans. Find out how much business you can do with a reasonable markup. Start making adjustments on items that are too low in price. Prices are still rising in your line, and the adjustments shouldn't be too difficult.

"Then, think about attracting some consumer trade. It might well provide as much as 25 percent of your volume before the end of the summer. Plan on some advertising. The local paper will help you lay out copy and figure costs.

"We'd like to help you stay in business in spite of your present ratios. Well—what do you say?"

As he rose to leave, Dave replied, "You know, Mr.

Tompkins, there's something about your approach that makes a lot of sense. Let me think the whole business through, for a few days, as I get more figures together. Then I'd like to map it out with you. Meanwhile, could you get started on that mortgage? It would give me some breathing space."

The banker nodded and the two walked to the door. In parting Dave remarked, "I think I can work it out. Heaven knows, I hope so." Then with a smile, "Maybe I'll turn out to be a good businessman after all. Anyway, thanks for the education on those revealing ratios!"

EVALUATING AND
INTERPRETING RATIOS

Putting ratios through their paces is likely to repay the time and effort many times over. Many a small business has been able to place operations on a sounder basis through examination of the relationships of margins and costs to sales, and by restoring balance to financial structure. Identification of a problem area can be made simpler with standards of attainable goals such as are provided by ratios. The first step in evaluating and interpreting ratios is establishing a point of view.

THE POINT OF VIEW

In comparing operating ratios for an individual concern with those of a given line of business, the business owner must realize that this comparison is made against averages. (Concede for the moment that these averages are typical; in other words, that the samples that afford the basis for the typical ratios are adequate and the compilations realistic.)

The first question, then, is this: Do you want to be just average? In this respect, the typical ratios are not par. They may include, but do not represent the performance of the least efficient and the most efficient firms in the sample. Hence the objective of the owner-manager should be to adjust operations so that they are at least as good as, but preferably better than, the typical operating ratios.

When dealing with balance-sheet ratios, the objective, again, is usually to do better than average. Here, though, the averages usually represent a boundary line of safety. A concern with all key ratios close to the proportions reflected by standard ratios for your line is not likely to get you into trouble.

A business may, of course, go below the average here or there, and from time to time. Its investment in fixed assets may be above average, for instance, but be offset by a high degree of liquidity of current assets. Or the fixed assets may be comfortably financed on a long term basis. Or again, a low rate of turnover of tangible net worth and working capital may be the result of an existing surplus of capital. Thus, a business doing $500,000 annual sales volume on a capital of $100,000 would show higher turnover, and somewhat greater financing problems, than a business doing the same volume with $200,000 in capital. The latter business could even show an above average ratio of fixed assets to tangible net worth, simply because it had not replaced its equipment with newer, more costly—but more efficient—machinery. The reverse situation, of course, could also develop.

Ratios are interrelated. That fact may be evaluated in terms of two fundamental precepts: Make money and stay solvent. They have a kinship with the three commandments of sound financial management mentioned earlier: Don't overbuy. Don't overtrade. And don't overexpand.

INTERPRETING
OPERATING RATIOS

The first step, of course, is to obtain whatever typical ratios are available. They need not always be absolutely up to date. Profit margins do not usually vary very widely from year to year. As a result, ratios of a few years back may be just as useful for initial comparisons as the very recent ratios which are much harder for the average small business owner to get. The objective is to set a starting point.

Once operating ratios are obtained, you will want to line them up on some sort of worksheet alongside an item-by-item column of your own results. Some combining of expense classifications may be necessary, but the major items should stand out.

Then comes the reduction of your own dollar operating figures to percents. Usually, a cost-of-doing-business survey will produce several sets of ratios, according to the dollar sales brackets, size of business, location, price class of merchandise, and similar factors. You will naturally want to make your comparisons according to the set ratios which fit your setup most closely.

After making a comparison, earmark those items in your own operating statement that appear seriously out of line with the trade average. Here, the first reaction may be to take some drastic step. However, more fitting would be a careful reflection as to the causes. You must know *why* your figures are out of line.

Selling expenses might be above average, for instance, because of special services to customers, compensated in turn by higher prices. Or a high-priced location could be compensated for by a better-than-average margin of gross profit. So each item should be considered in relation to the overall return.

Once these comparisons are analyzed, corrective steps in proportioning expenses to sales may be worked out. Such measures are not necessarily negative. Some managers may see ways to improve their showings by *adding* expenses. For example, perhaps the former advertising budget was too low. An increase might bring in more income.

In this connection, it is essential to understand some of the significant influences on major classifications of the operating statement.

COST OF GOODS SOLD AND GROSS MARGIN

Cost of goods sold and gross margin are definitely inter-related. Costs may, for example, appear high because the margin is too low. Cost of goods sold may be higher or lower than that shown by a typical ratio for several reasons.

One reason for higher cost of goods may be inventory write-downs. If inventories are high during a period, and closing inventories must be valued below original cost at inventory time, the closing inventory will be lower than normal and will affect cost of goods.

The cost of goods may be too high because of wasteful buying practices. In a manufacturing business, inefficient labor will affect the cost of converting raw materials into finished products, as will excessive overhead.

Cost of goods also may seem high simply because of a comparatively low selling price. For example: If sales are $50,000 and cost of goods is $40,000, then gross profit on sales is 20 percent and cost of goods sold is 80 percent. But if gross profit were arbitrarily increased to 25 percent while cost of goods stayed the same, sales would be $53,300, and the $40,000 figure would represent only 75 percent of sales.

Gross profit, then, may rise or fall because of what affects the costs of goods sold. When your gross profit is seriously out of line with prevailing averages, it is a good idea to examine your buying costs and pricing structure. If the gross profit is higher, it may be a logical result of location, extra services, and the like, the cost of which must be offset by selling prices.

Cost of goods sold is also related to inventory valuations. If, for example, closing inventory is overvalued, gross profit will increase—and vice versa.

OPERATING EXPENSES

Wages and Salaries

Labor cost is a major item among operating expenses in the profit-and-loss account. The reaction of a business owner to how others in the line are managing these expenses will be instinctive.

A number of ratio studies provide interesting supplementary data for analyzing wage-cost relationships. Some studies, for instance, show a breakdown of *sales per employee*. Other studies which do not make this breakdown may nevertheless show figures for typical dollar sales and dollar expenditures. In this event—if the number of employees is given—the ratio of dollar sales per employee may be computed and compared with figures for your own business.

The latter relationship would be particularly interesting in comparing *selling costs*. Many sales managers have now come to review selling costs with great care. An abnormally high selling cost-to-sales ratio may lead to questions about selling efficiency. A very low selling cost-to-sales ratios may make it worthwhile to find out whether the selling effort is being concentrated in skimming the cream of large volume customers, and whether a profitable segment of a sales territory represented by smaller volume buyers is being neglected.

At the same time, it is also possible that out-of-line sales costs may be due not so much to the inefficiency of the sales force as to sales and promotion methods. Many retailers have installed self-service departments in their stores as a means of improving their sales-to-cost ratios.

Owner's Compensation

The salaries of management are another item worthy of analysis. In a proprietorship or partnership, for instance, it is often the practice to compute profits before allowing for any compensation to owner or owners. Whatever earnings are left, after all other deductions, represent their compensation. Some businessmen feel that every concern should be charged with the expense of a manager. The owner, they say, would have to employ an outside manager if he or she did not exercise that function. In this connection, typical operating ratios can give some insight into the size of the salary an owner should draw for being manager. It should, of course, be noted that some ratios are distorted to the extent that they combine corporation figures with those of partnerships and proprietorships.

When management compensation is too high as compared with the prevailing standard, it may indicate that an excessive part of profits, which should be retained for future growth, is being drained from the business. Such a procedure is really inviting trouble—for every business should create some kind of cushion, either for expansion or to meet unforeseen contingencies. Some businesses, of course, will be exceptions because they have available to them a liberal surplus of capital over their needs. Moreover, there are profitable concerns in today's highly competitive market, which are content to stand pat on their present volume of business.

In some instances, too high a ratio of management compensation to other items may suggest that the business is supporting too many principals. A store once operated by two partners might become less attractive as a business venture if, say, four or five partners were to start drawing from it.

Attention should also be called to the situation in which officer-owners of closely held corporations prefer to take their compensation as salaries rather than in dividends. This approach can have a very marked influence on the management payroll.

Advertising Cost

Improperly used, of course, advertising may prove to be something less than a cure for competitive problems. The incident may be recalled of a small manufacturer of underwear who spent relatively large sums to bring its product before the public. The advertising was in good taste, and the campaign was well planned. Sales did go up. But so much capital had been laid out in publicity that the business was unable to pay its bills. It went bankrupt before earnings could catch up. The point is that advertising outlays must be subjected to careful planning just as are other costs.

Occupancy Cost

Every dollar paid in rent should bring a proportionate return in income. If location costs are high in relation to sales, they should be offset by correspondingly higher prices. Many "swanky stores" located on "exclusive thoroughfares" take this principle for granted.

Perhaps the ratio of occupancy to sales may be a little misleading as the sole arbiter of whether or not rent costs are in line. While this is a useful standard for comparison, it is good to compute also the ratio of *rent to gross profit*. The latter is overlooked in most typical ratio studies, but you can compute and compare it from basic data in the studies.

Bad Debt Costs

Credit is an instrument of sales. The manufacturer or wholesaler who does not grant credit is a rarity. Credit granting is becoming increasingly in vogue among retailers. There's money in it. Some grocers, such as those specializing in home deliveries and high-priced items, find that through credit, they are able to obtain higher profit margins. In other instances, while the markup cannot be increased, the credit risk is offset by larger volume.

Nevertheless, the manager who becomes deliberately careless about granting credit is asking for trouble. Faulty reasoning is all too easy. Take, for instance, the manager of a small retail business who was being swamped with orders from new credit accounts on Saturday mornings. This manager was in a quandary for fear that "If I ask them to fill our credit applications, I'll drive the customers away!"

INTERPRETING
BALANCE-SHEET RATIOS

Many business executives have not schooled themselves to the significance of financial balance in their business. As an operating executive, you very likely tend to concentrate on your income account in seeking ways to increase profits or reduce losses. Nevertheless, a careful review of your balance sheets is a worthwhile related procedure. A knowledge of the distribution of your assets and liabilities and an appreciation of the typical ratios for the more successful concerns in your line or area can be of great value. It is particularly so in judging whether the financial structure of your company should be altered or redesigned to improve operating performance.

If the operating statement shows signs of progress, it is easy to rationalize a bad situation, which could be corrected, by saying, "We don't have enough capital," or even "Let the creditors carry us for awhile; look at the business we give them."

All too often, slow payments are an end result of unhealthy underlying conditions that may ultimately endanger the business. You might find, for example, overstocked inventories, excessive collection periods, ill-thought-out expansion programs, or too large investments in fixed assets. In the course of the existence of most concerns there are peaks in business activity, followed by valleys. In the ensuing fluctuations in prices and sales, some unbalanced concerns are unable to make the adjustment. There is always a chance of trouble developing as the result of some unforeseen event such as the advent of new technology or a shift in style. If liabilities are heavy, real difficulties will certainly be faced. A business must have reserves for almost any emergency.

CURRENT ASSETS TO CURRENT LIABILITIES

In the evolution of financial analysis, it early on became a practice to compare current assets to current liabilities. The beginning and the end of financial analysis in those days was the expectation that a healthy business would have a margin of $2 in current assets to $1 in current debts. This, it was said, could be considered as "an infallible guide." That notion was not to last for long.

Later, there evolved a second simple comparison: the sum of the cash and receivables to the total of current liabilities.

Still later, a third modification in elementary analysis occurred. Some readers may recall that certain credit issuers, even bankers, upon receiving a balance sheet for credit consideration, would mentally write down the receivables to a valuation of 75 percent of the figure shown on the statement, while also mentally writing down the inventories by 50 percent. These write-downs were made on the theory that these assets were probably overstated to begin with, and that the write-down probably represented what the assets would bring under forced liquidation. Credit, if extended at all, would be granted only on the basis of the "revised" asset values.

However, experience has proved that no single ratio can possibly give a complete picture of financial condition. Other facts can be of vital significance, each telling its own story in conjunction with related ratios and conditions in the particular business.

Nevertheless, a current ratio *does* tell a story. It *is* an item of evidence. But it should be used with judgment. Sometimes the story is deceptive. A 4-to-1 ratio in a seasonal business might go down to 1.5-to-1 at the height of the season. Or it might be high because of large amounts of accumulated unsold inventory. In the apparel trades, it is always important to consider how much of a "carryover" exists from one season to the next; for instance, summer dresses on hand in the autumn. In this regard, a shoe store in Brooklyn had a current ratio of 4 to 1 largely because of a stock of $20,000 in high button shoes—which would never be sold.

A 2-to-1 current ratio is not necessarily a guarantee of sound financial condition, but it's not a bad idea to have one most of the time. Ratios below that figure occasionally prevail in the food industry, or among concerns that have exceptionally fast turnovers of receivables and inventories. Most managers will recognize that a current ratio less than 2 to 1 is a symptom of possible trouble. It's an outward sign that financial stress is occurring.

LIABILITIES TO TANGIBLE NET WORTH

Beware of topheavy liabilities! If they do nothing else, they undermine business judgment. Managers who are worried about finding money to meet obligations are less likely to have the analytical objectivity they need to plan sound programs for their businesses.

One of the best indicators of top-heavy liabilities is the relationship of liabilities to tangible net worth. A small business is unlikely to owe much in the way of term loans, debentures, or bonds. Term debts are more likely to be loans from officers. These are internal, and in the opinion of many creditors are the most dangerous kind of debt. Or they may be mortgage loans secured by real estate or equipment. If these are large, then the ratio of total debt to tangible net worth may prove significant.

How much can a concern afford to owe? Some analysts feel that for most small manufacturing concerns, a debt equivalent to 75 percent of tangible net worth is pretty high. When liabilities exceed that figure, they reason, the equity of creditors in the assets is coming too close to equaling the equity of the owners. For the small retail business, they would argue that current liabilities should seldom come to more than 50 percent of tangible net worth. Why? A retailer, they note, usually has most current assets in inventory, which must be sold to realize cash. A heavily obligated retailer may find a sudden letdown in inventory turnover embarrassing.

There are only three ways to reduce debt. *One* is to invest more capital—not always available. The *second* is to liquidate assets—not always practical. The *third* is to build up capital from earnings—not possible overnight. So watch those debts.

TURNOVER OF TANGIBLE NET WORTH AND WORKING CAPITAL

When capital is forced to turn over too rapidly, a series of consequences sets in. Every dollar is tied up in some phase of operations. Every cog in the business machine has to function perfectly because there is no reserve of money which can be called upon in an emergency. There can be no letdown in orders received and in sales transacted. Receivables must be collected promptly; a large bad debt becomes fatal because that money was essential to pay bills.

The more a firm's inventory needs replenishment, the more rapid its rate of buying. Bills accumulate. Money has to be borrowed and these loans have to be repaid. What if there are cancellations, or strikes, or marketing changes, or if customers just stop buying? That is where liabilities begin to take on dangerous momentum.

NET PROFITS ON TANGIBLE NET WORTH

In 1928 and 1929, radio manufacturing was tremendously profitable. One particular manufacturer made over $5 million in net profits in a single year, on an initial capital of about the same amount. A 100 percent net profit on capital in one year is very heady wine. Next year, the entire capital, including last year's profit, was spent in enlarging the plant. Then, the following year, the bottom fell out of radio and the company went broke.

When net profits loom large in relation to tangible net worth over a very short period, they can lead to a very warm self-appreciative glow. They are like meat to a hungry hunter, and they lure plenty of wolves out of the forests of competition.

There is not much need to belabor the issue of net profits that are too low in relation to capital.

No one has ever proved how much a concern should earn on its existing capital. Nevertheless the fact remains that business ought to make a reasonable return on the money invested in it. That return should be adequate to compensate for risk and provide incentive. After all, profit is the payoff.

AVERAGE COLLECTION PERIOD

Not many concerns could afford to cut off every overdue customer. Some of these customers provide volume—and they do not all fail. A random survey of one hundred concerns rated as "fair" credit risks ten years ago would find that most of them are still in business.

Credit management implies selectivity. Credit management by rigid yardsticks is pretty cumbersome. Too lax a credit policy can turn credit into a bog, an unsafe footing for business sales. Too rigid a policy can mean loss of business and a failure to cultivate future profitable outlets.

The collection period is a medium for comparison; it doesn't pinpoint the condition of individual accounts. If the collection period is too high, it may mean deadwood in the receivables in the form of accounts that should be written off. It might even be a signal that nonbusiness receivables, such as loans to outsiders, are included. Slow collections could be a danger signal of overdependence on too many slow payers. Too low a collection period might justify taking a few more credit risks.

So watch average collection periods—your own, and the other person's.

INVENTORY TURNOVER

One owner spent a spring vacation in the West and combined business with pleasure by buying his entire summer's requirements from western factories. Prices were high, and he had many a happy vision of what profits would accrue from higher prices which were bound to come that summer. Apparently he never asked himself, "But what if prices go down?"

Actually, he would have been put out of business, because those commitments exceeded his capital, and he had borrowed the money with which to buy. Fortunately, prices did not decline, but they didn't go up either.

Many a marginal business has remained alive because of unexpected profits that accrued from appreciation of inventories in the rising market. The trouble is that sometimes those unexpected profits come to be accepted as a normal return from "astute" management. However, unexpected losses from inventory depreciation in a falling market have just as often become a prelude to bankruptcy for such self-acknowledged astute entrepreneurs.

An excessive inventory can result in unexpected losses from depreciation, changes in style, perishability, and price fluctuations. A typical small business will seldom find it desirable to carry more than 100 percent of its working capital in inventory.

The profits a business earns are justified by risks taken in the normal function of converting goods from raw materials to finished products, of distributing goods, of judging style and anticipating demand, of stocking goods to suit customer convenience, and of rendering services. Net profits for such functions are seldom spectacular. In other words, the legitimate function of a business is to merchandise, produce or serve—not to speculate. Speculative profits and losses are for speculators. Business owners may be entitled to speculate, if they can afford it, but they cannot afford it on creditors' money.

FIXED ASSETS TO TANGIBLE NET WORTH

Once there was a manufacturer of what, for the sake of protecting the company, must be called "widgets." The business was started in a very small way, but the owner was quite ingenious. The widgets were unusual in that they were completely processed, whereas competing products required further operations before use. Moreover, these particular items were being produced at a comparatively low price. The demand was great. The manufacturer began to expand rapidly.

From an output of a few widgets a day, production grew until, in two years, it was up to 10,000 widgets a week. That was the absolute maximum; it took new machinery to accomplish that. At this point, a big customer said, "Why don't you put in an assembly line—we will take all the widgets we can get." Money was borrowed and still more machinery was installed. Production went up to 30,000 units a week. The problem was that it took all the money the owner could get to equip the new plant.

One day, the plant manager called the owner and said, "We're running low on materials. Send us more raw widgets."

The owner had to reply, "Can't—haven't any money to buy them."

Whereupon the plant's operation had to be cut back to about one-half its capacity. This was expensive because depreciation and maintenance were heavy. Payments to suppliers became very slow. Days were anxiety-filled. Only through intensive efforts was the manager able to get outsiders to recognize sufficient profit possibility to invest additional capital and put the business back on its feet. The costs of maintenance, repairs, and depreciation could have wiped out the equity.

The point to remember is that fixed-asset requirements are relative. For example, they are high for a motor carrier and a canner, low for a cotton goods converter, a wholesaler, or an average retailer. For an average small business, if fixed assets exceed 75 percent of worth, they may become unmanageable because bills cannot be paid with brick and mortar. When money is borrowed to put into fixed assets, the borrowings become a kind of mortgage on future earnings or new capital. For only earnings or new capital can repay that kind of debt. Meanwhile, maturing debt installments may become troublesome.

MANAGEMENT
JUDGMENT NECESSARY

No statistical study will substitute for management judgment. Ratios cannot give the final answer to questions of operating policy. They cannot convert every enterprise into a success overnight. They can help in measuring performance. The knowledge of what others in the same line are doing can be of real assistance in making decisions and in locating potential trouble areas. Beyond that, small business owners and managers must look to themselves for effective action.

9

LOOKING AHEAD

As your business grows, there will probably be times when you will need additional funds for investment or operations. You must be able to plan for these requirements, and to do this you will need forecasting tools.

The techniques described in this chapter—the cash budget and projected financial statements (sometimes called "pro forma" statements)—serve many purposes. They help you to keep last-minute decisions and surprises at a minimum, to set standards of performance for various activities of your business, to anticipate financial needs and the effects of policy changes. They are a valuable aid in discussions with prospective lenders. They help you answer such questions as these:

- Will I need additional money?

- When will I need it?

- How long will I need it?

- How much do I need?

- Where can I get it?

- How much will it cost?

- If I borrow it, how can I repay it?

THE CASH BUDGET

The cash budget is simply a plan for cash receipts and expenditures during a given period. It is one of the most valuable financial tools at your disposal. By figuring out your cash needs and cash resources ahead of time, you put yourself in a better position to:

- Take advantage of money-saving opportunities such as economic order quantities, cash discounts, and so on.

- Make the most efficient use of cash.

- Finance your seasonal business needs.

- Develop a sound borrowing program.

- Develop a workable program of debt repayment.

- Provide funds for expansion.

- Plan for the investment of surplus cash.

How To Do It

The length of the period to be covered by the cash budget depends on the nature of your business, how ample your supply of cash is, and how regularly cash flows into and out of your business. The form shown in Exhibit 16 is for a simple cash budget prepared monthly.

The groundwork for preparing a cash budget consists of estimating all cash receipts and cash payments expected during the budget period. Budgets must be carefully planned for cash sales (including discounts and sales returns and allowances), payments of accounts receivable, and any other expected cash income. The same kind of planning must be done for each type of expense that will go to make up the expected cash expenditures. These budgets are based on experience and on the goals you have set for your business.

If expected cash receipts total more than expected cash payments, the difference is added to the expected cash balance at the beginning of the period. If payments total more than receipts, the difference is subtracted. In either case, the result is the expected cash balance at the end of the period.

The cash balance—how much is enough? You must also decide what size cash balance you need to maintain. This, too, is based on experience. You might, for instance, decide that cash equivalent to a certain number of days' sales is a desirable level. If the cash balance at the end of the budgeted period is less than this amount, some short-term borrowing or changes in plans may be necessary. The cash budget, by bringing this to your attention early, gives you time to consider fully all the possible courses of action.

If, on the other hand, the cash balance is larger than you need, the excess can be temporarily invested in marketable securities.

If you need funds—what kind? Cash budgets can help you decide whether you need short-term or long-term capital. A series of twelve monthly cash budgets will show your estimated monthly cash balances for a year. Each of these balances can then be compared with the cash level you have established as desirable for your business. Perhaps your cash balance is ample at the beginning and end of the twelve-month period but low at times during the year. This suggests a need for short-term funds. The need will be self-liquidating over the twelve-month period.

If, however, cash budgets are developed over longer periods of time and the cash balance is consistently low, the business needs intermediate or long-term capital—inter-

EXHIBIT 16

Cash Budget

Cash Budget
For Three Months Ending March 31, 19—

	January		February		March	
	Budget	**Actual**	**Budget**	**Actual**	**Budget**	**Actual**
Expected cash receipts:						
1. Cash sales						
2. Collections on accounts receivables						
3. Other income						
4. Total cash receipts						
Expected cash payments:						
5. Raw materials (or merchandise)						
6. Payroll						
7. Other direct factory expenses						
8. Advertising						

9. Selling expense _____

10. Administrative expense _____

11. Plant and equipment _____

12. Other payments (taxes, Interest, and so on) _____

13. Total cash payments _____

14. Expected cash balance at beginning of month _____

15. Cash increase or decrease (item 4 minus item 13) _____

16. Expected cash balance at end of month (item 14 plus item 15) _____

17. Desired cash balance _____

18. Short-term loans needed (item 17 minus item 16 if item 17 is larger) _____

19. Cash available for short-term investment (item 16 minus item 17 if item 16 is larger) _____

mediate if the need persists for periods lasting from twelve to thirty months, and long-term or permanent capital if it persists for a longer period.

PROJECTED FINANCIAL STATEMENTS

The cash budget deals with only one account—cash. It is useful to carry your plans for the future a step further by drawing up a profit-and-loss statement and a balance sheet. These statements record your best estimates of what the profitability of your business will be during the period covered and the financial condition of the business at the end of the period. They should be drawn up at least quarterly; and if your business is short of funds, you would be wise to prepare them more often. They will help you avoid unforeseen peak needs that might prove embarrassing.

By providing a look into the future of your business, projected financial statements enable you to judge what the financial needs of your business will be at the end of the forecast period. You can then plan ahead of time whatever steps may be needed to strengthen the business or to prepare for future growth. If you wait until the need actually arises, it will be more difficult and may even be too late.

The Projected Profit-and-Loss Statement

The value of the projected profit-and-loss statement as a guide depends largely on your estimate of sales during the period for which the projection is being made. It is therefore well worth your time to develop this estimate as accurately as possible. Use the past experience of the business, figures provided by salespeople, management projections, and any other useful information.

Next, the cost of goods sold must be estimated. A useful first step is to analyze operating data to find out what percentage of sales has gone into cost of goods sold in the past. This percentage can then be adjusted for expected variations in costs, price trends, and efficiency of operations. (A more detailed method estimates each cost item separately and totals the results.)

Other expenses, other income, and taxes can also be estimated on the basis of past experience and expected changes.

A typical projected profit-and-loss statement for the Titan Manufacturing Company is shown in Exhibit 17.

The Projected Balance Sheet

The projected balance sheet is a summary of the results expected at the end of the period for which the projection is being made. It shows the effect on each balance-sheet item of the sources and uses of funds planned in the various budgets.

- The *cash figure* appearing on the projected balance sheet (see Exhibit 18) is the amount decided on as the desirable cash balance in the cash budget. The Titan Company has established 15 days' sales as their desired cash balance. On the basis of the sales estimate of $80,000 for December (Exhibit 17), the cash account would be $40,000 on their projected balance sheet.

- The *receivables* and *inventory accounts* can be based on past experience and estimated sales. Assume that Titan's receivables have averaged 30 days' sales in the past, and that inventories have been turning over roughly

EXHIBIT 17

Profit-and-Loss Statement of a Manufacturing Company

Titan Manufacturing Company[1]
Projected Profit-and-Loss Statement
for the Month Ending December 31, 19—

		Figures based on:
Revenue from sales............	$80,000	Sales budget for the month
Cost of sales............	56,000	Experience (for Titan, 70 percent of sales)
Gross margin............	$24,000	
Operating expenses:		
Selling expenses............ $10,200		Budget for the month
General expenses............ 4,000		Experience (for Titan, $2,400 fixed costs plus variable costs of 2 percent of sales)

Total operating expenses	14,200	
Net income from operations	$9,800	
Other expense:		
Interest expense	500	Outstanding debt
Net profit before taxes	$9,300	
Income taxes	2,790	Tax rate of 30 percent
Net profit after taxes	$6,510	
Earnings withdrawn	5,000	Owner's intention
Retained earnings	$1,510	

¹Not a real company.

EXHIBIT 18

Balance Sheet of a Manufacturing Company

Titan Manufacturing Company
Projected Balance Sheet
December 31, 19—

Current assets:

Cash	$40,000	Desired cash balance equal to 15 days' sales
Accounts receivable	80,000	Average collection period of 30 days' sales
Inventory	160,000	Monthly turnover of ½ during this season
Total current assets	**$280,000**	
Fixed assets	500,000	Present figure adjusted for month's depreciation.
Total assets	**$780,000**	

Liabilities

Current Liabilities:

Notes payable	$69,000	Amount of borrowed funds needed to balance assets
Accounts payable	76,000	Expectation of 60 days' purchases on the books
Accrued liabilities	11,000	Same as preceding period
Total current liabilities	$156,000	
Long-term debt	70,000	Unchanged
Total liabilities	$226,000	

Equity

Paid-in capital	$350,000	Unchanged
Retained earnings	204,000	Present amount plus earnings to be retained in December
Total equity	554,000	
Total liabilities and equity	**$780,000**	

one-half times monthly. If other conditions and policies do not change, with Titan's sales estimate of $80,000, receivables should be about $80,000 and inventory $160,000 at the end of the month.

- *Fixed assets* on the estimated balance sheet are based on earlier fixed-asset accounts. That is, the accounts on the most recent balance sheet are adjusted for depreciation and expected additions to or reduction in these assets.

- *Accrued liabilities* and *long-term debts* can usually be assumed to remain unchanged. Of course, if your experience has been that accrued liabilities tend to vary with sales volume, you should take this into account. Any expected increase or reduction in long-term debts during the period should also be given effect.

- The *accounts payable figure* is based on an estimate of the number of days' purchases that will be outstanding at the end of the month. Recent and expected purchases and your creditors' terms of sale must be considered.

- The *equity account* consists of the existing ownership account plus the earnings to be retained during the period. The amount of retained earnings to be added here comes from the projected income statement. The remaining account, *notes payable*, is the last to be computed (unless it has already been determined in connection with the cash budget). Notice that without it, the combined equity and liabilities ($711,000) fall $69,000 short of the total assets ($780,000). This indicates that if the estimates used were reasonably accurate, Titan will need roughly $69,000 of borrowed funds to finance the activities planned.

Points to Remember

Bear in mind two characteristics of projected financial statements. *First*, these statements can be built up in a number of ways. The best approach is to rely on whatever information is fairly easy to get together and enables you to make the most accurate estimates for the various accounts. *Second*, remember that these statements are based on estimates and assumptions. They provide only a rough sketch of what may happen.

If actual performance differs widely from the estimates at any point however, the reason should be sought. Was the estimate unrealistic, or were there weaknesses in your company's performance at that point? Whichever proves to be the case, the trouble spot should be attended to.

LOOKING STILL
FURTHER AHEAD

You may find it hard to estimate capital requirements in the more distant future by developing projected cash budgets and financial statements. Business expectations twenty-four months ahead, for instance, may be too uncertain for detailed schedules to be pieced together.

In such cases, ask yourself this question: "Do I expect to do the same volume of business two years from now, or do I expect to do *x* percent more business?" When you have the answer to that question, you can make a rough estimate of your capital requirements for the period. Here's how.

Examine past financial statements to find the normal cash, inventory, accounts receivable, accounts payable, and short-term borrowing *per dollar of sales*. Then multiply these amounts by the dollar sales volume you expect to be doing in two years. Add to existing fixed assets any additions you expect to make during the two years.

You are now well on your way to constructing a rough projected balance sheet for that time. A concluding step is to subtract total estimated liabilities from total estimated assets. The difference is the projected equity account.

Now compare this account with your existing equity account. The difference between the two will have to be made up by retained earnings plus growth capital.

THE DIFFERENT TYPES
OF FINANCING

In this chapter we will discuss distinctions among the three different types of financing: (1) equity capital, (2) working capital, and (3) growth capital. This distinction is important since you must first know the exact nature of what it is you need in order to obtain adequate financing.

Equity capital is the cornerstone in the financial structure of any company. Equity is technically that part of the balance sheet which reflects ownership of the company. It also represents the total value of the business since all other financing amounts to some form of borrowing which must ultimately be repaid. When a lending officer asks the question "What do you have in the business?" he is asking about your equity. Equity capital is not generally obtainable from institutions—at least not during the early stages of business growth. By way of distinction, working capital and growth capital can be obtained in a number of ways. Both become necessary when equity capital has been used to the limit of its availability. The working capital and growth capital extend the effectiveness of equity by providing the leverage on investment present in the financial picture of most successful businesses.

Working capital needs arise as a result of the ongoing activities of the business. Funds are required to carry accounts receivable, to obtain inventories, and to meet payroll. It is to satisfy such needs that working capital is required. In most businesses the magnitude of these needs vary during the year and it is the varying use of more or less money to finance these requirements during the business cycle which most quickly identifies this funding requirement as working capital.

Growth capital although frequently grouped together with working capital, is different in that this funding source is not directly related to the cyclical aspects of the business. Instead, growth capital is usually involved when the business is expanding or being altered in some significant way. Usually the change in the business can be expected to result in higher levels of general profitability and cash flow, and it is because of this change that various types of growth capital can be arranged. Rather than looking for seasonal liquidity or reducing this type of borrowing as in the case of working capital, lenders which make growth capital available frequently depend on increased profits to provide orderly repayment of such loans over a longer period of time.

The need for the presence of all three types of capital—equity capital, working capital, and growth capital—continues in every growing business. You should not expect a single financing program maintained for a short period of time to eliminate every future need.

As prospective suppliers of financing begin to analyze the requirements of your business, they will begin to distinguish among the three functional types of capital in the following way: (1) fluctuating (working capital), (2) amortizing (growth capital), and (3) permanent (equity capital).

If you are asking for a *working capital* loan, you will be expected to show how the loan can be reduced during your business's period of greatest liquidity during the business cycle or over a one-year period. If you seek *growth capital*, you will be expected to show how these moneys will be used to make your business more profitable and generate extra cash which can be used to repay the loan over several years.

If, on the other hand, you are not asking for either working or growth capital, it is likely that a lender will say to you "we would like to be of assistance but we cannot invest in your business—this is the role of equity capital and we only make loans." This is a natural and quite logical response for a bank cannot be expected to become "locked in" with its money obtained from depositors as would a stockholder or a private investor whose amount of moneys are placed at risk for dividend return or future capital gains.

With this background in mind, we can now begin to explore the various types of working capital loans and the sources which make this type of financing available to small businesses.

The Small Business Administration (SBA) is an independent agency of the Federal Government, established by Congress to advise and help the Nation's small businesses. Its major areas of activity are:

- Serving as advocate for small business within the federal government.

- Providing management assistance and encouraging private sector financing of small business.

- Promoting business development and capital ownership among minorities and women.

- Helping small business get a fair share of government procurement contracts and subcontracts.

SBA LOANS

If borrowing does appear to be necessary or advisable, and if no private source can be found, SBA can guarantee up to 90 percent of a local bank loan. However, by law, SBA cannot consider a loan application unless there is evidence that the loan could not be obtained elsewhere on reasonable terms without SBA assistance.

SBICS AND OTHER VENTURE CAPITAL SOURCES

Small Business Investment Companies (SBI's) are licensed and financed by the Small Business Administration (SBA) for the purpose of providing venture capital to small business concerns. This capital may be in the form of secured and/or unsecured loans, debt securities with equity characteristics, or "pure" equity securities which are represented by common and preferred stock.

Venture capital is extremely difficult to define; however, it is characterized as being high risk with the principal objective of capital gains. The structure and terms of the financing are responsive to the needs of the small business rather than to the requirements of the venture investors. Additionally, and probably more importantly, venture capital is characterized by a continuing active relationship between the small business and the venture capitalist.

WHEN TO TURN TO VENTURE CAPITALISTS

If your business requires additional equity capital and if internally available moneys are simply inadequate, some form of venture capital participation may make sense. Venture capitalists will expect a relatively high percentage of ownership in your company for a given amount of money initially invested in the business. At the same time these financiers may provide invaluable assistance in lining up additional outside financing, marketing and product ideas, and general management consulting.

It is important for you to recognize that you are taking on a partner who will maintain an active interest in your business and its direction when you become involved with venture capitalists. They can provide guidance and open many doors, and they are generally patient and sympathetic to the problems associated with building a small business. They are usually prepared to wait longer than the average investor for profits to arrive so long as you are conscientiously pursuing your objectives. Most venture capitalists expect a 15 percent rate of return on their investment or higher and expect to see profits within a five- to seven-year period.

UNSECURED BORROWINGS FOR WORKING CAPITAL

Chapter 3 defined working capital as the difference between current assets and current liabilities. To the extent that your working cash balances, cash accounts receivable, and inventories exceed trade credit—the gap must be financed. The simplest means of obtaining this working capital is by borrowing on an unsecured basis. Commercial banks are the largest source of this type of financing which has the following basic characteristics:

1. The loans are short-term but renewable.

2. They fluctuate according to seasonal needs or follow a fixed schedule of reduction or amortization.

3. The loans call for periodical repayment.

4. They have no lien on any assets of the borrower.

5. They usually require that all indebtedness of the borrowing company to its principals be subordinated.

6. They have no priority over any common creditor of the borrower.

7. They are granted primarily in ratio to the net current assets (working capital) position of the borrower.

Commercial banks usually prefer unsecured loans even though they do not include liens. This is because the loans are least costly to handle and administer. At the same time the banks grant unsecured credit only when they feel that the general liquidity and overall financial strength of your business relative to the size of the credit provide ample ability for repayment.

You may be able to predict that you require working capital financing for a specified interval, say 3 to 5 months, in which case the bank can issue a credit with that specific term. Most likely, however, your working capital need will continue over the cyclical growth pattern of your business. As suggested in the previous chapter, the usual function of working capital is to supplement the role of equity in connection with fluctuating needs over a period of the business cycle. Therefore, most unsecured credits are established on a year's basis and set up on the bank records as such. Despite the fact that a one-year credit is established, the bank is likely to continue handling the transaction with a series of renewable 90-day notes. Theoretically, at 90-day intervals the bank will reappraise the credit situation and can conceivably call your note asking for repayment in full. In actual practice the bank is likely to feel that it has screened the credit with sufficient care in the beginning to review only once a year. Therefore, the 90-day maturity date is only a technicality; however, you must handle it properly by paying it off in cash on or before due date or, usually, "paying by renewal."

Although most unsecured loans fall into the category just described—that is, the one-year line of credit consisting of a series of renewable 90-day notes—there is another type of working capital loan which is also frequently used. This is the amortizing loan which calls for a fixed program of reduction usually on a monthly or quarterly basis. If you borrow for working capital purposes on an amortizing basis, your bank is likely to agree to terms longer than a year so long as you comply with the schedule of stipulated principal reductions.

There is an important feature to the types of borrowing arrangements described above. Namely, while a loan commitment from a bank for working capital can only be negotiated for a relatively short term, after satisfactory performance during that term the arrangement can be continued indefinitely on the assumption that a good business relationship exists between you and your bank and that your credit-worthiness has not been impaired.

"THE ANNUAL CLEAN-UP"

Once a year the bank will expect you to pay off your unsecured borrowings for perhaps 30 or 60 days and this is what is known as *"the annual clean-up."* This clean-up occurs during the period of greatest liquidity during the year when it is possible for your indebtedness to be at its lowest level. This normally occurs following a seasonal sales peak when inventories have been reduced and receivables are largely collected from customers prior to the beginning of a new business buildup.

You may discover that it becomes progressively more difficult to repay debt or "clean-up" and this condition usually occurs due to the following reasons: (1) your business is growing to the extent that this year's period of least activity represents a considerable increase over the corresponding period of the previous year, (2) you are increasing your immediate short-term capital requirement because of some new promotional program or addition to operations, or (3) you are experiencing a reduction in profitability and cash flow which, hopefully, is temporary in nature.

Frequently, such a condition will justify a combination of both open line "self-liquidating" financing and the amortizing type of unsecured borrowing. For example, you might try to arrange a combination of perhaps $15,000 of open line credit to handle peak financial requirements during the business cycle and at the same time $20,000 of amortizing unsecured borrowings to be repaid at a rate of say $4,000 per quarter. In appraising such a request for combination of unsecured loans, your commercial bank, if it is on its toes, will insist on an explanation based on past experience and future projection for both: (1) how the $15,000 of open line credit will be self-liquidating during the year with ample room for the annual clean-up and (2) how, as a result of increased profits and resulting cash flows, you can be expected to meet the schedule of amortization on the $20,000 portion.

Since unsecured loans provide no prior claim or lien on assets to the lender, you have to provide ample assurances as to liquidity and to overall financial health to qualify for this type of financing. Credit acceptability is usually based on the following: (1) debt-to-worth ratio and (2) net current asset position. In many instances debt-to-worth ratios of 2 to 1 or even 3 to 1 are quite acceptable. Beyond that limit, however, other financing techniques may have to be used. With regard to your net current asset position, banks normally limit their unsecured open lines to 40 percent or 50 percent of working capital, sometimes going a little higher to allow for seasonal peaks. Still other banks in appraising the suitability of an unsecured line focus on the current ratio as a rough index of liquidity and for most types of businesses an acceptable current ratio is 1.5 to 1.

PUTTING YOUR
BEST FOOT FORWARD

It is important to present your company's case persuasively to the bank if you are to succeed in obtaining unsecured credit lines. You should have a financial plan which contains a cash budget for the next 12 months as well as a pro forma balance sheet and income statement. You should be prepared to explain fully how these statements have been prepared and the underlying assumptions on which the figures are based. Obviously, these assumptions should be supportable. One final reminder. Many banks prefer that statements be prepared by an outside accountant and submitted on his or her stationery. Perhaps it is sometimes unjustified, but the outside accountant or financial adviser frequently has additional credibility as the result of professional experience with financial matters and familiarity with many businesses. Only you can judge whether the assistance of an outsider will be useful in negotiations with your commercial banker.

12

SECURED WORKING
CAPITAL FINANCING

Your company may have reached the point where it is ineligible for additional unsecured borrowing arrangements with a commercial bank. This may be because your bank has reached its lending limit or takes the view that additional unsecured credit cannot be extended.

Under the circumstances it may be possible to arrange for your bank to participate with a commercial finance company in offering a secured credit which may result in a more advantageous interest rate than would be obtainable with a straightforward secured lending program.

The principal distinction between unsecured lending discussed in the previous chapter and secured borrowing is the existence of a lien—that is, a prior claim on specific assets given by the borrower to the lender. Under the Uniform Commercial Code which has been adopted by all 50 States, all classes of liens today are now lumped together under the term "security interests" which forms the basis for a security agreement. The presence of the lien means that common creditors and trade suppliers cannot look to the value of certain assets for repayment except subject to the claims of lienholding lenders.

ACCOUNTS RECEIVABLE FINANCING

The most common form of secured financing involves liens against accounts receivable. This type of financing is offered both by commercial banks and commercial finance companies. While distinctions are made by lenders among industry and individual firms, advances can usually be obtained amounting from 70 percent to 90 percent of outstanding quality receivables. Usually an "open limit" is established which permits the amount of financing to fluctuate as your receivable portfolio grows or declines.

Although the stated interest charge may be higher than for unsecured bank borrowings, the actual money cost differential between secured and unsecured borrowing may not be so high as it initially appears. This is due to the fact that secured borrowing costs are usually calculated based on actual cash used by the borrower on a daily basis and interest charges computed in this fashion may prove more moderate in comparison with unsecured borrowing costs which usually involve compensating balance requirements with the costs not included in the stated interest rates.

FACTORING

As noted, accounts receivable financing involves borrowing with your accounts receivable as collateral. In factoring, unlike accounts receivable financing, the receivables are actually purchased by the factor without recourse. This non-recourse arrangement is normally limited, however, to the credit risk and the factor is protected against circumstances that would invalidate sales. Factoring is logical when it makes sense for outside parties to assume the responsibility for follow-up and collection. Traditionally, factors are used in industries where they have better firsthand knowledge of customers and their creditworthiness than do the sellers and where as a consequence, they can be more effective in converting the accounts receivable into cash.

Secured working capital financing can also be obtained by *pledging inventories*. In some instances inventories are stored in public warehouses where disinterested third parties having no affiliation with the borrower can provide protection for the associated lenders. A variation used by many companies for inventory financing involves field warehousing in which a clearly delineated area is set aside on the premises of the buyer enabling a disinterested third party to take full responsibility for the inventory against which credits are extended. Depending on the nature of your business and conditions in your industry, it may be possible to obtain a 60 percent to 75 percent advance with inventory as a lien.

13

SECURED GROWTH CAPITAL FINANCING

Lenders assume that working capital loans—whether extended on a secured or an unsecured basis—will be repaid through the automatic liquidation of receivables and inventories during the course of the business cycle. Thus, it is the inherent liquidity of the business rather than overall profitability that supports such borrowing programs. By way of contrast, growth capital loans are extended for longer periods of time and are repaid from profits rising from business activities extending several years into the future. It is logical, therefore, that growth capital loans are secured by collateral that remains unchanged in the possession of the borrower, that is, the noncurrent of fixed assets such as machinery and equipment.

In working capital financing primary credit emphasis is placed on the quality of collateral. For growth capital lending stress will be placed on underlying rationale for the borrowing. In other words, you will need to demonstrate that growth capital can be used to increase cash flows or sources of payment through increased sales, cost savings, or greater production efficiencies. Although your building, equipment, or machinery will probably be the collateral for growth capital borrowing, the use of the funds is not necessarily restricted to purchase of additional equipment. Any general business purpose is eligible as long as it promises possibilities of success.

Although you may wish to borrow to acquire a specific piece of new equipment if substantial amounts of growth capital are involved, the lender is likely to insist that all machinery and equipment of the business be pledged and the percentage of the advance is likely to range somewhere between 25 percent and 57 percent of the equipments' book value.

LEASING

For a particular piece of new equipment it may be possible to arrange a lease in which case you will not actually own the equipment, but rather enter into an arrangement where your firm obtains exclusive use of it over a specified number of years. Such an arrangement may have possible tax advantages besides releasing funds which would otherwise be tied up in ownership of the equipment.

CONDITIONAL SALES PURCHASES

Still another variation involves purchasing equipment on a time payment basis. Naturally, the ownership of the property under such an arrangement is retained by the seller until the buyer has made all the required monthly or quarterly payments over the term of the contract.

SALE LEASEBACKS

Most purchased leases involve new equipment. It is some-times possible to sell equipment that your business owns to a leasing company and then lease it back. It may be possible under such an arrangement to obtain an advance equal to or larger than what could be obtained through a conventional mortgage arrangement.

PULLING THE VARIOUS ELEMENTS TOGETHER

Many business situations are best financed by a combination of the various types of credit arrangements described earlier. For example, your business may qualify for secured bank credit extended on a regular 90-day renewable basis as long as it is possible to "clean-up" or "rest" the line annually. If the short-term, liquidating facet of your financial require-ment is separated from the longer-term components, this may indeed be possible. The longer-term components are more likely to be accommodated by some form or combi-nation of types of secured financing. Receivables financing and warehouse lending may be possibilities and these, in turn, may be supplemented by chattel mortgage borrowing or one of the other forms of borrowing against fixed assets. Commercial finance companies are well qualified to help you develop a proper solution in the use of secured financing options together with unsecured borrowings.

14

FOR FURTHER INFORMATION

This book has described several concepts and tools of financial analysis that can help the small business owner-manager interpret financial data and manage the operations of his business. But it is important to remember that understanding and applying these tools successfully requires more than a knowledge of how the tools work. It is also essential to understand when the tools should be used and, more important, what their strengths and limitations are.

Financial analysis cannot be carried out in a routine, standardized way. You must be able to tailor the concepts and tools to the specific requirements of your business. You must ask yourself, "What questions need to be asked about my business?" and then, "What approach shall I use to get practical answers to these questions?"

Before analyzing a financial problem, ask yourself these questions:

- "What factors, trends, relations, and time periods have a bearing on the problem?"

- "What tool or method of analysis will be most useful?"

- "How much detail work is justified?"

The amount of literature in the field of business finance is vast. Some of the information is not applicable to the finance problems of small businesses. Much of it is, however, and some of it is designed especially for small business.

The following lists may be useful to small business owner-managers who wish to study the subject of business finance further. The lists are necessarily brief. No slight is intended toward authors and sources not included.

SOURCES OF INDUSTRY RATIO DATA

Among the best known sources of industry ratio data with which to compare your own ratios are the following:

- *Key Business Ratios*. Published annually by Dun and Bradstreet, Inc., 99 Church St., New York, NY 10007. Covers 125 lines of business activity, including manufacturing, wholesaling, retailing, and construction.

- *Statement Studies*. Published annually by Robert Morris Associates, National Association of Bank Loan Officers and Credit Men, Philadelphia National Bank Building, Philadelphia, PA 19107.
  Based on data collected from member banks. Covers approximately 300 lines of business.

- *Specialized Industry Reports*. There are many sources of ratio data specializing in single industries or industry groups. These sources include trade associations, specialized accounting firms, trade magazines, universities, some larger industrial corporations, and several governmental agencies. A number of them are listed in the booklet *Ratio Analysis for Small Business* (see below, under "U.S. Publications"). This booklet also has more detailed information about the publications whose specific titles are mentioned above.

U.S. GOVERNMENT PUBLICATIONS

The following publications may be purchased from the Superintendent of Documents, Washington, D.C. 20402. Write for current price and availability.

Cost Accounting for Small Manufacturers (SBMS No. 9). U.S. Small Business Administration.

Ratio Analysis for Small Business (SBMS No. 20). U.S. Small Business Administration.

Guides for Profit Planning (SBMS No. 25). U.S. Small Business Administration.

Financial Control by Time-Absorption Analysis (SBMS No. 37). U.S. Small Business Administration.

Buying and Selling a Small Business (Nonseries). U.S. Small Business Administration.

BOOKS

Entrepreneurship and Venture Management. Clifford M. Baumback. 1983. Prentice-Hall, Inc., Englewood Cliffs, NJ 07632.

Guide to Buying or Selling a Business. James M. Hansen. 1983. Prentice-Hall, Inc., Englewood Cliffs, NJ 07632.

How to Run a Small Business. J. K. Lasser Tax Institute. 1984. McGraw-Hill Book Company, Inc., 1221 Avenue of the Americas, New York, NY 10020.

Small Business Management Fundamentals. Dan Steinhoff, 1984. McGraw-Hill Book Company, Inc., 1221 Avenue of the Americas, New York, NY 10020.

How to Start Your Own Business. William D. Putt. 1984. MIT Press, 28 Carleton St., Cambridge, MA 02142.

Guide to Venture Capital Sources. Stanley M. Rubel. 1982. Capital Publishing Corp., Two Laurel Ave., Wellesley Hills, MA 02181.

Handbook for Manufacturing Entrepreneurs. Robert S. Morrison. 1983. Western Reserve Press, Inc., Box 675, Ashtabula, OH 44004.

APPENDIX

SOURCES OF
RATIO STUDIES

Ratio study sources may be classified into three groups. First are agencies that compile data for a number of industries as a by-product of their major function. Among the best known of these are Dun & Bradstreet, Inc., the Robert Morris Associates, and the Accounting Corporation of America. Second is the large number of trade associations which, often in conjunction with colleges or universities, compile studies of the various trade groups and industries with which they are associated. Third are various agencies and departments of the federal government.

In addition, a few industrial companies conduct ratio studies in their customer lines for the benefit of their clients. Among these are Eli Lilly, the National Cash Register Corporation, and Eastman Kodak.

DUN & BRADSTREET, INC.

Since 1932, Dun & Bradstreet has been publishing "Key Business Ratios" in the monthly, *Dun's Review*. These financial ratios cover 22 retail, 32 wholesale, and 71 industrial lines of business. Dun & Bradstreet also annually compile *Cost of Doing Business*, operating ratios extracted from data in the Internal Revenue Service's *Statistics of Income*. These are published and distributed by Dun & Bradstreet and are available from their Public Relations Department, 99 Church Street, New York, New York 10007 or at any of their branches.

The following types of businesses are covered in financial and operating ratio studies issued by Dun & Bradstreet:

Key Business Ratios

Retailing

Auto and home supplies
Children's and infants' wear stores
Clothing and furnishings, men's and
  boys'
Department stores
Discount stores
Discount stores, leased departments
Family clothing stores
Furniture stores
Gasoline service stations
Grocery stores
Hardware stores
Household appliance stores
Jewelry stores
Lumber and other building materials
  dealers
Miscellaneous general merchandise
  stores
Motor vehicle dealers
Paint, glass and wallpaper stores
Radio and television stores
Retail nurseries, lawn and garden
  supply dealers
Shoe stores
Variety stores
Women's ready-to-wear stores

Wholesaling

Air conditioning and refrigeration
  equipment and supplies
Automotive equipment
Beer, wine and alcoholic beverages
Chemicals and allied products
Clothing and accessories, women's
  and children's
Clothing and furnishings, men's and
  boys'
Commercial machines and
  equipment
Confectionery
Dairy products
Drugs, drug proprietaries, and
  sundries
Electrical appliances, TV and radio
  sets
Electrical apparatus and equipment
Electronic parts and equipment
Farm machinery and equipment
Footwear
Fresh fruits and vegetables
Furniture and home furnishings
Groceries, general line
Hardware
Industrial machinery and equipment

Lumber and construction materials
Meats and meat products
Metals and minerals
Paints, varnishes, and supplies
Paper and its products
Petroleum and petroleum products
Piece goods
Plumbing and heating equipment
and supplies
Poultry and poultry products
Scrap and waste materials
Tires and tubes
Tobacco and its products

Manufacturing and Construction

Agricultural chemicals
Airplane parts and accessories
Bakery products
Blast furnaces, steel works and
rolling mills
Blouses and waists
Books, publishing and printing
Broad woven fabrics, cotton
Canned and preserved fruits and
vegetables
Commercial printing except
lithographic
Communication equipment
Concrete, gypsum and plaster
products
Confectionery and related products
Construction, mining and handling
machinery and equipment
Converted paper and paperboard
products
Cutlery, hand tools and general
hardware
Dairy products
Dresses
Drugs
Electric lighting and wiring
equipment

Electric transmission and
distribution equipment
Electrical industrial apparatus
Electrical work
Electronic components and
accessories
Engineering, laboratory and
scientific instruments
Fabricated structural metal products
Farm machinery and equipment
Footwear
Fur goods
General building contractors
General industrial machinery and
equipment
Grain mill products
Heating and plumbing equipment
Heavy construction, except highway
and street
Hosiery
Household appliances
Industrial chemicals
Instruments, measuring and
controlling
Iron and steel foundries
Knot outerwear mills
Malt liquors
Mattresses and bedsprings
Meat packing plants
Metal stampings
Metalworking machinery and
equipment
Millwork
Miscellaneous machinery, except
electrical
Motor vehicle parts and accessories
Nonferrous foundries
Office and store fixtures
Office computing and accounting
machines
Outerwear, children's and infants'
Paints, varnishes, lacquers and
enamels
Paper mills, except building paper
Paperboard containers and boxes

Passenger car, truck, and bus bodies
Petroleum refining
Plastics, materials, and synthetics
Plumbing, heating and air
  conditioning
Sawmills and planing mills
Screw machine products
Shirts, underwear, and nightwear,
  men's and boys'
Soap, detergents, perfumes, and
  cosmetics
Soft drinks, bottled and canned
Special industry machinery
Suits and coats, women's and
  misses'

Suits, coats, and overcoats, men's
  and boys'
Surgical, medical, and dental
  instruments
Toys, amusement and sporting
  goods
Trousers, men's and boys'
Underwear and nightwear, women's
  and children's
Wood household furniture and
  upholstered
Work clothing, men's and boys'

Cost of Doing Business

Retailing

Apparel and accessories
Automotive dealers
Building materials, hardware, and
  farm equipment
Drug and proprietary stores
Eating and drinking places
Food stores
Furniture and home furnishings
Gasoline service stations
General merchandise
Liquor stores

Wholesaling

Alcoholic beverages
Drugs
Dry goods
Electrical goods
Farm products
Groceries
Hardware, plumbing, and heating
  equipment

Lumber and construction materials
Machinery
Metals and minerals
Motor vehicles
Paper and its products
Petroleum and its products

Manufacturing

Apparel
Chemicals and allied products
Electrical supplies and equipment
Fabricated metal products
Food products (bakery products,
  beverage industries, canned
  goods, dairy products, grain mill
  products, meats, and sugar)
Furniture and fixtures
Leather and its products
Lumber and wood products
Machinery
Motor vehicles and equipment
Ordnance, except guided missiles
Paper and allied products
Petroleum refining

Primary metal industries
Printing and publishing
Rubber and miscellaneous plastics
  products
Scientific industries
Stone, clay, and glass products
Textile mill products
Tobacco
Transportation equipment

**Services, Transportation, and
Communication**

Advertising
Air transportation
Automobile parking, repair, and
  service
Business services
Electrical companies and systems
Gas companies and systems

Hotels
Medical services
Motion picture production
Motion picture theaters
Personal services
Pipeline transportation
Radio and television broadcasting
Railroad transportation
Repair services
Telephone and telegraph services
Trucking and warehousing
Water supply and other sanitary
  services
Water transportation

**Finance, Insurance, and Real
Estate**

Agriculture and Mining

ROBERT MORRIS ASSOCIATES

Long noted among the banking fraternity for extensive work
in the field of ratio compilation and analysis is Robert Morris
Associates, a national association of bank loan and credit
officers. Founded in 1914, this organization's size is indicated by the fact that its membership comprises more than
1,200 commercial banks. Its activities include maintenance
and advancement of standards of correct credit practice.

Robert Morris Associates has developed ratio studies
for over 350 lines of business as indicated below. Owners
and managers of small concerns wishing further information
on the availability of this material may address inquiries to
the Executive Manager, Robert Morris Associates, Philadelphia National Bank Building, Philadelphia, Pennsylvania

19107. Following is a list of lines of business for which Robert Morris Associates provides ratios:

Manufacturing

Advertising displays and devices
Apparel and other finished fabric
    products:
  Canvas products
  Children's clothing
  Curtains and draperies
  Men's, youths', and boys' suits,
    coats, and overcoats
  Women's dresses
  Women's suits, skirts, sportswear,
    and coats
  Women's undergarments and
    sleepwear
Beverages:
  Flavoring extracts and syrups
  Malt liquors
  Wines, distilled liquor, and
    liqueurs
Caskets and burial supplies
Chemicals and allied products:
  Drugs and medicines
  Fertilizers
  Industrial chemicals
  Paint, varnish, and lacquer
  Perfumes, cosmetics, and other
    toilet preparations
  Plastics and synthetic resins
  Soap, detergents, and cleaning
    preparations
Food and kindred products:
  Bread and other bakery products
  Candy and confectionery supplies
  Canned and dried fruits and
    vegetables
  Dairy Products
  Flour and other grain mill
    products

  Frozen fruits, fruit juices,
    vegetables, and specialties
  Meat packing
  Prepared feeds for animals and
    poultry
  Vegetable oils
Furniture and fixtures:
  Mattresses and bedsprings
  Metal household furniture
  Store, office, bar, and restaurant
    fixtures
  Wood furniture—except
    upholstered
  Wood furniture—upholstered
Jewelry, precious metals
House furnishings
Leather and leather products:
  Footwear
  Furs
  Hats
  Men's and boys' sport clothing
  Men's work clothing
  Men's, youths', and boys'
    separate trousers
  Men's, youths', and boys' shirts,
    collars, and nightwear
  Luggage and special leather
    products
  Tanning, currying, and finishing
Lumber and wood products:
  Millwork
  Prefabricated wooden buildings
    and structural members
  Sawmills and planing mills
  Veneer, plywood, and hardwood
  Wooden boxes and containers
Machinery, equipment, and
    supplies—electrical:
  Air conditioning

Electronic components and accessories

Equipment for public utilities and industrial use

Machinery, except electrical equipment:

Ball and roller bearings

Construction and mining machinery and equipment

Farm machinery and equipment

General industrial machinery and equipment

Industrial and commercial refrigeration equipment and complete air conditioning units

Machine shops—jobbing and repair

Machine tools and metal working equipment

Measuring, analyzing, and controlling instruments

Oil field machinery and equipment

Special dies and tools, die sets, jigs, and fixtures

Special industry machinery

Metal industries—primary:

Iron and steel forgings

Iron and steel foundries

Non-ferrous foundries

Metal products—fabricated (except ordnance, machinery, and transportation equipment):

Coating, engraving, and allied services

Cutlery, hand tools, and general hardware

Enameled iron, metal sanitary ware, and plumbing supplies

Fabricated plate ware

Fabricated structural steel

Heating equipment, except electric

Metal cans

Metal doors, sash, frames, molding and trim

Metal stampings

Miscellaneous fabricated wire products

Miscellaneous non-ferrous fabricated products

Screw machine products, bolts, nuts, screws, rivets, and washers

Sheet metal work

Valves and pipe fittings, except plumbers' brass goods

Paper and allied products:

Envelopes, stationery, and paper bags

Paperboard containers and boxes

Pulp, paper, and paperboard

Printing, publishing, and allied industries:

Book printing

Bookbinding and miscellaneous related work

Books: publishing

Commercial printing, lithographic

Newspapers: publishing and printing

Periodicals

Typesetting

Rubber and miscellaneous plastics products:

Miscellaneous plastics products

Rubber footwear and fabricated rubber products

Stone, clay, and glass products:

Brick and structural clay tile

Concrete brick, block, and other products

Minerals and earths, ground or otherwise treated

Pressed and blown glass and glassware

Ready-mixed concrete

Textile mill products:
  Broad woven fabric—cotton, silk, and synthetic
  Broad woven fabric—woolens and worsteds
  Dyeing and finishing
  Hosiery—anklets—children's, men's and boys'
  Hosiery—women's—full fashioned and seamless
  Knitting—Cloth, outerwear and underwear
  Narrow fabrics and other smallwares
  Yarn—cotton, silk, and synthetic
Toys, amusement, sporting and athletic goods:
  Games and toys, except dolls and children's vehicles
  Sporting and athletic goods
Transportation equipment:
  Aircraft parts (except electric)
  Motor vehicle parts and accessories
  Motor vehicles
  Ship and boat building and repairing

Wholesaling

Automotive equipment and supplies:
  Automobiles and other motor vehicles
  Automotive equipment
  Tires and tubes
Beauty and barber supplies and equipment
Drugs, drug proprietaries and druggists' sundries
Electrical equipment:
  Electrical supplies and apparatus
  Electronic parts and supplies
  Radios, refrigerators, and electrical appliances
Flowers and florists' supplies
Food, beverages, and tobacco:
  Coffee, tea, and spices
  Confectionery
  Dairy products and poultry
  Fish and sea foods
  Frozen foods
  Fruits and vegetables
  General groceries
  Grains
  Meats and meat products
  Tobacco and tobacco products
  Tobacco leaf
  Wine, liquor, and beer
Furniture and home furnishings:
  Floor coverings
  Furniture
General merchandise
Iron, steel, hardware and related products:
  Air conditioning and refrigeration equipment and supplies
  Hardware and paints
  Metal products
  Metal scrap
  Plumbing and heating equipment and supplies
  Steel warehousing
Lumber, building materials, and coal:
  Building materials
  Coal and coke
  Lumber and millwork
Machinery and equipment:
  Agricultural equipment
  Heavy commercial and industrial machinery and equipment
  Laundry and dry cleaning equipment and supplies
  Mill supplies
  Professional equipment and supplies

Restaurant and hotel supplies,
fixtures and equipment
Transportation equipment
and supplies, except
motor vehicles
Paper and paper products:
Printing and writing paper
Wrapping or coarse paper and
products
Petroleum products:
Fuel oil
Petroleum products
Scrap and waste materials:
Textile waste
Sporting goods and toys
Textile products and apparel:
Dry goods
Footwear
Furs
Men's and boys' clothing
Women's and children's clothing
Wool

Retailing

Aircraft
Apparel and accessories:
Family clothing stores
Furs
Infants' clothing
Men's and boys' clothing
Shoes
Women's ready-to-wear
Boat dealers
Books and office supplies:
Books and stationery
Office supplies and equipment
Building materials and hardware:
Building materials
Hardware stores
Heating and plumbing equipment
dealers
Lumber

Paint, glass, and wallpaper
stores
Cameras and photographic supplies
Department stores and general
merchandise:
Department stores
Dry goods and general
merchandise
Drugs
Farm and garden equipment and
supplies:
Cut flowers and growing plants
Farm equipment
Feed and seed—farm and garden
supply
Food and beverages:
Dairy products and milk dealers
Groceries and meats
Restaurants
Fuel and ice dealers:
Fuel, except fuel oil
Fuel oil dealers
Furniture, home furnishings, and
equipment:
Floor coverings
Furniture
Household appliances
Radio, Television, and record
players
Jewelry
Liquor
Luggage and gifts
Motor vehicle dealers:
Autos—new and used
Gasoline service stations
Mobile homes
Motorcycles
Tires, batteries, and accessories
Trucks—new and used
Musical instruments and supplies
Road machinery equipment
Sporting goods
Vending machine operators,
merchandise

Services

Advertising agencies
Automobile repair shops
Automobile and truck rental and
    leasing
Bowling alleys
Cable television
Car washing
Commercial research and
    development laboratories
Data processing
Direct mail advertising
Engineering and architectural
    services
Farm products warehousing
Funeral directors
Insurance agents and brokers
Intercity bus lines
Janitorial services
Laundries and dry cleaners
Linen supply
Local trucking
Local trucking—without storage
Long distance trucking
Motels, hotels, and tourist courts
Nursing homes
Outdoor advertising

Photographic studios
Radio broadcasting
Real estate holding companies
Refrigerated warehousing, except
    food lockers
Refuse systems
Telephone communications
Transportation on rivers and canals
Travel agencies
Television stations
Water utility companies

Contractors

Not Elsewhere Classified

Beef cattle raisers
Bituminous coal mining
Bottlers—soft drinks
Commercial feed lots
Construction, sand and gravel
Crude petroleum and natural gas
    mining
Horticultural services
Poultry, except broiler chickens
Seed companies (vegetable and
    garden)

ACCOUNTING CORPORATION OF AMERICA

The Accounting Corporation of America publishes semi-annually the *(Mail-Me-Monday) Barometer of Small Business*. Its data are derived as a by-product of the Accounting Corporation's accounting services to clients throughout the country.

The *(Mail-Me-Monday) Barometer* classifies its operating ratios for the various industry groups on the basis of gross volume. The classifications vary with the industry group but seldom exceed $300,000. The emphasis is on small business.

The ratios can be obtained from the Accounting Corporation's Research Department, 1929 First Avenue, San Diego, California 92101.

Following is a list of types of business for which there are ratios:

Apparel, children's and infants	Laundromats and hand laundries
Apparel, men's specialty	Laundries, plant
Apparel, men's and women's	Liquor stores
Apparel, women's specialty	Lumber and building material
Appliance stores	Machine shops
Auto parts and accessories	Meat markets
Bakeries	Motels
Beauty shops	Music stores
Cocktail lounges	New car dealers
Confectionery stores	Nursery and garden supplies
Contractors—building	Paint, glass, and wallpaper
Contractors—specialty	Photographic supply stores
Dairies	Plumbing and heating equipment
Dentists	Printing shops
Doctors of medicine	Professional—others
Dry cleaning shops	Repair services
Drug stores	Restaurants
Feed and seed stores	Service stations
Florists	Shoe stores
Food stores—combination	Sporting goods stores
Food stores—specialty	Taverns
Furniture stores	TV radio sales and service
Garages	Transportation
Gift and novelty stores	Used car dealers
Hardware stores	Variety stores
Jewelry stores	

NATIONAL CASH REGISTER COMPANY

The National Cash Register Company publishes an annual "Expenses in Retailing." This booklet examines the cost of operation in about forty lines of business. The ratios are obtained from primary sources, most of which are trade associations. For some lines of business, the expense percentages are broken down into "controllable expense" and "fixed expense." Following is a list of businesses covered in a recent NCR study:

Apparel stores
Appliance and radio-TV dealers
Automobile dealers
Auto parts dealers
Beauty shops
Book stores
Building material dealers
Cocktail lounges
Department stores
Dry cleaners
Feed stores
Florists
Food stores
Furniture stores
Garages
Gift, novelty, and souvenir stores
Hardware stores
Hotels
Jewelry stores

Laundries
Liquor stores
Mass merchandising stores
Meat markets
Men's wear stores
Motels and motor inns
Music stores
Novelty stores
Nursery and garden supply stores
Photographic studio and supply stores
Professional services
Repair services
Restaurants
Service stations
Shoe stores (family)
Sporting goods stores
Supermarkets
Transportation and service
Variety stores

THE BANK OF AMERICA

As a service to business owners and managers and students of small business, as well as to those thinking about starting a small firm, the Bank of America periodically issues detailed studies of problems in opening a business. These studies, published in its *Small Business Reporter*, include costs-of-doing-business ratios. They can be obtained by writing to *The Small Business Reporter*, Department 3120, P.O. Box 37000, San Francisco, California. Titles of issues in recent years include:

Apparel Stores
Auto Parts
Bars
Bicycle Stores
Book Stores
Building Maintenance Services
Independent Camera Stores
Proprietary Day Care Centers
Independent Drug Stores
Coin Operated Dry Cleaning Stores
Business Equipment Rental
Convenience Food Stores
The Handicraft Business
Health Food Stores

Home Furnishing Stores
Independent Liquor Stores
Mail Order Enterprises
Mobile Home and Recreation Dealers
Independent Pet Shops
Plant Shops
Small Job Printing Shops
Repair Services
Restaurants and Food Services
Service Stations
Sewing and Needlecraft Shops
Shoe Stores
Independent Sporting Goods
Toy and Hobby Craft Stores

SPECIALIZED INDUSTRY SOURCES

The most important specialized industry sources for ratio data are trade associations. In addition, however, accounting firms, trade magazines, universities, and some large companies publish ratio studies.

TRADE ASSOCIATIONS

National associations which have published ratio studies in the past include the following:

American Association of Advertising Agencies, 200 Park Avenue, New York, New York 10019
American Camping Association, Bradford Woods, Martinsville, Indiana 46151
American Meat Institute, 1600 Wilson Boulevard, Arlington, Virginia 22209
American Paper Institute, 260 Madison Avenue, New York, New York 10016
American Society of Association Executives, 1101 16th Street, N.W., Washington, D.C. 20036
American Supply Association, 221 North LaSalle Street, Chicago, Illinois, 60601
Bowling Proprietors Association of America, Box 5802, Arlington, Texas 76011
Building Owners and Managers Association, International, 224 South Michigan Avenue, Chicago, Illinois 60601

Door and Hardware Institute, 1815 North Fort Meyer Drive, Suite 412, Arlington, Virginia 22209

Florists' Transworld Delivery Association/Interflora, 29200 Northwestern Highway, Southfield, Michigan 48076

Foodservice Equipment Distributors Association, 332 South Michigan Avenue, Chicago, Illinois 60604

Laundry and Cleaners Allied Trades Association, 543 Valley Road, Upper Montclair, New Jersey 07043

Material Handling Equipment Distributors Association, 104 Wilmot Road, Deerfield, Illinois 60015

Mechanical Contractors Association of America, 5530 Wisconsin Avenue, N.W., Suite 750, Washington, D.C. 20015

Menswear Retailers of America, 390 National Press Building, Washington, D.C. 20043

Motor and Equipment Manufacturers' Association, 222 Cedar Lane, Teaneck, New Jersey 07666

National American Wholesale Grocers' Association, Room 1810, 51 Madison Avenue, New York, New York 10010

National Appliance and Radio-TV Dealers Association, 318 West Randolph Street, Chicago, Illinois 60606

National Art Materials Trade Association, 182 A Boulevard, Hasbrouck Heights, New Jersey 07604

National Association of Accountants, 919 Third Avenue, New York, New York 10022

National Association of Electrical Distributors, 600 Madison Avenue, New York, New York 10022

National Association of Food Chains, 1725 Eye Street, N.W., Washington, D.C. 20006

National Association of Furniture Manufacturers, 8401 Connecticut Avenue, Suite 911, Washington, D.C. 20015

National Association of Insurance Agents, Inc., 85 John Street, New York, New York 10038

National Association of Music Merchants, Inc., 35 East Wacker Drive, Chicago, Illinois 60601

National Association of Plastics Distributors, 472 Nob Hill Lane, Devon, Pennsylvania 19333

National Association of Retail Grocers of the United States, Suite 620, 2000 Spring Road, Oak Brook, Illinois 60521

National Association of Textile and Apparel Wholesalers, Statler-Hilton Hotel, 33rd Street and Seventh Avenue, New York, New York 10001

National Association of Tobacco Distributors, 58 East 79th Street, New York, New York 10021

National Automatic Merchandising Association, 7 South Dearborn Street, Chicago, Illinois 60603

National Beer Wholesalers Association of America, 6310 North Cicero Avenue, Chicago, Illinois 60646

National Confectioners Association of the United States, 36 Wabash Avenue, Chicago, Illinois 60603

National Consumer Finance Association, 1000 16th Street, N.W., Washington, D.C. 20036

National Decorating Products Association, 9334 Dielman Industrial Drive, St. Louis, Missouri 63132

National Electrical Contractors Association, Inc., 7315 Wisconsin Avenue, 13th Floor, Washington, D.C. 20014

National Electrical Manufacturers Association, 155 East 44th Street, New York, New York 10017

National Farm and Power Equipment Dealers Association, 2340 Hampton Avenue, St. Louis, Missouri 63139

National Home Furnishings Association, 405 Merchandise Mart Plaza, Chicago, Illinois 60654

National Kitchen Cabinet Association, 334 East Broadway, Louisville, Kentucky 40202

National Lumber and Building Material Dealers Association, 1990 M Street, N.W., Washington, D.C. 20036

National Machine Tool Builders Association, 7901 Westpark Drive, McLean, Virginia 22101

National Office Products Association, 1500 Wilson Boulevard, Arlington, Virginia 22209

National Oil Jobbers Council, Inc., 1750 New York Avenue, N.W., Washington, D.C. 20006

National Paint and Coatings Association, 1500 Rhode Island Avenue, N.W., Washington, D.C. 20005

National Paper Box Association, 231 Kings Highway East, Haddonfield, New Jersey 08033

National Paper Trade Association, Inc., 420 Lexington Avenue, New York, New York 10017

National Parking Association, 1101 17th Street, N.W., Washington, D.C. 20036

National Restaurant Association, One IBM Plaza, Suite 2600, Chicago, Illinois 60611

National Retail Hardware Association, 964 North Pennsylvania Avenue, Indianapolis, Indiana 46204

National Retail Merchants Association, 100 West 31st Street, New York, New York 10001

National Shoe Retailers Association, 200 Madison Avenue, New York, New York 10016

National Soft Drink Association, 1101 16th Street, N.W., Washington, D.C. 20036

National Sporting Goods Association, 717 Michigan Avenue, Chicago, Illinois 60611

National Tire Dealers and Retreaders Association, 1343 L Street, N.W., Washington, D.C. 20005

National Wholesale Druggists' Association, 670 White Plains Road, Scarsdale, New York 10583

National Wholesale Hardware Association, 1900 Arch Street, Philadelphia, Pennsylvania 19103

National Wholesale Jewelers Association, 1900 Arch Street, Philadelphia, Pennsylvania 19103

Northamerican Heating and Airconditioning Wholesalers Association, 1661 West Henderson Road, Columbus, Ohio 43220

North American Wholesale Lumber Association, Inc., Box 713, Clifton, New Jersey 07013

Northeastern Retail Lumbermens Associations, 339 East Avenue, Rochester, New York 14604

Optical Wholesalers Association, 6935 Wisconsin Avenue, Washington, D.C. 20015

Painting and Decorating Contractors of America, 7223 Lee Highway, Falls Church, Virginia 22046

Petroleum Equipment Institute, 1579 East 21st Street, Tulsa, Oklahoma 74114

Printing Industries of America, Inc. 1730 North Lynn Street, Arlington, Virginia 22209

Scientific Apparatus Makers Association, 1140 Connecticut Avenue, N.W., Washington, D.C. 20036

Shoe Service Institute of America, 222 West Adams Street, Chicago, Illinois 60606

Society of the Plastics Industry, Inc., The, 355 Lexington Avenue, New York, New York 10017

Super Market Institute, Inc., 303 East Ohio Street, Chicago, Illinois 60611

United Fresh Fruit and Vegetable Association, 1019 19th Street, N.W., Washington, D.C. 20036

Urban Land Institute, 1200 18th Street, N.W., Washington, D.C. 20036

Wine and Spirit Wholesalers of America, Inc., 7750 Clayton Road, Suite 201, St. Louis, Missouri 63117

GOVERNMENT SOURCES

Federal government publications provide a wealth of data covering somewhat broader industry classifications in most cases than the private sources.

Among these are the Federal Trade Commission, the Interstate Commerce Commission, the United States Department of Commerce, the United States Department of

Agriculture, the Civil Aeronautics Board, the Federal Communications Commission, the Federal Power Commission, and—notably—the Securities and Exchange Commission.

The Internal Revenue Service of the United States Treasury Department annually publishes *Statistics of Income*. This volume contains income statement and balance sheet data compiled from U.S. income tax returns.

Finally, the *Census of Business*, published at five-year intervals by the Bureau of the Census, provides limited ratio and dollar financial information.

OTHER SOURCES

A number of accounting and management consulting firms have done or are doing ratio studies in selected lines of business. Such work has been done in the hotel, restaurant, home furnishings, laundry, and dry cleaning industries. In addition, various trade publications conduct ratio studies from time to time.

Two well-known industrial companies, the Eli Lilly Company (drugs) and the Eastman Kodak Company (photography), are particularly noted for their data on retail operations in their industries.

INDEX

ABOUT THE AUTHOR

Ronald Spurga has worked as an investment banker and securities analyst on Wall Street since 1975. He is currently vice president of a multinational financial services institution.

Mr. Spurga has a BA from Rutgers University and an MBA in Finance and a PhD in Economics from Fordham University. Besides his professional duties, he serves as an adjunct professor at New York University's Graduate School of Business Administration.

In addition to *Balance Sheet Basics,* Mr. Spurga has written a best-selling investment primer entitled *A Practical Guide to the Commodities Markets.*